A Journey of a Thousand

A memoir of cancer, courage, and a little bit of crazy

LAURA L. ZICK-MAUZY

Print ISBN: 979-8-35095-251-3

Cover design by
http://topbookdesigner.weebly.com/

Printed in the United States of America, 2024 on SFI-certified paper

Disclaimer

This book is a memoir. It depicts events in the author's life as truthfully as recollection permits. The names of some persons were changed to respect their privacy, and characteristics were changed. Some events were compressed, and some dialogue was recreated. All persons noted within are actual individuals; there are no composite characters.

The information contained in this book is for informational purposes only. No material within is intended to substitute for professional medical advice, diagnosis, or obtaining treatment.

This story was not AI-generated. It contains flaws because the author is flawed. It is raw and real, unpretentious and unique.

**This book is dedicated to every person
touched by the horror of cancer.**

The survivors.

The caregivers.

The families, friends, and the medical community.

In loving memory of:

My mother, REBECCA ZICK (1935-2015)
the strongest woman I have ever known
BREAST CANCER AND THYMUS CANCER

JOHN DAVIS (1956-1997)
my first love
ACUTE LYMPHOCYTIC LEUKEMIA

My mother-in-law, RUTH MAUZY (1931-1987)
sadly, she passed before I met Paul
COLON CANCER

My brother-in-law, MIKE MAUZY (1954-2012)
Unfortunately, I never met Mike
SOFT TISSUE SARCOMA

My friend, DAVID MARTIN (1948-2022)
a dear friend and faithful cheerleader (he, coincidentally, was at the
cancer center the day I had my first appointment)
METASTATIC LUNG CANCER

<u>Acknowledgments</u>

First and foremost, I want to thank God for His unwavering Love and Mercy. He's my Rock, my Strength, my Deliverer, my Everything.

- I'd also like to sincerely thank my sisters, Ann, Jeanie, and Janie, and my best friend, Donna, for their unwavering support throughout my journey. Your encouragement and belief in me have been invaluable.

- I want to give a huge thanks to my sons for their empathy, acceptance, patience, and sense of humor. You two are the reason I fought.

- It's an honor to recognize my surgical healthcare team. Dr. Ridgely, I wouldn't likely be alive today without your exceptional surgical expertise, profound understanding of the human anatomy, compassion, and unwavering commitment to serving your patients.

- My team at the cancer center was also dedicated to my physical, emotional, and healing needs. I felt supported by everyone from the moment I walked in the door, and I never felt rushed because I was beyond my "allotted time." I felt *heard.*

- And finally, I want to express my heartfelt gratitude to my remarkable husband, Paul, without whose steadfast support, continuous gentle motivation, and continued encouragement, this book would not have come to fruition.

- Jean Bee, my beta reader, is my longtime friend and avid reader. I am shocked that someone I genuinely admire agreed to read for me. I know it was a lot of hours and I hope you don't regret it! I appreciate you more than you know!

- Eliska Hahn Diller, we were destined to meet. Your talents impress me more every day, and even though I've tried to dislike you, I just can't. <<smiling from ear to ear>> You are authentic and beautiful, inside and out. Thank you for being my voice and my heart on the audiobook.

- Special thanks to Current Medical Technologies, Inc. for giving me written permission to use their product information and image. Your product helps so many women.

CONTENTS

INTRODUCTION

" But she doesn't have cancer anymore. She's just gonna have to suck it up and get it done." A coworker shared this shocking and cold statement that one of the supervisors made about me. Even more surprising was that this occurred in the healthcare industry, where I was employed. Healthcare. Where professionals care about your health. Upon learning this, I experienced mixed emotions — hurt, astonishment, and anger. It was difficult to comprehend: How could someone exhibit such a strong sense of judgment?

Of course, I realized that the individual likely had no personal understanding or experience with the dreadful disease; however, he was an educated and empathetic individual. But not on this day.

After a while, I considered that most people are unfamiliar with these things. As a result, I concluded that the average person only understands what they've personally encountered or been educated about. After much thought, I determined that I needed to share my story.

If you have ever felt like physicians use ambiguous jargon to muddle the unpleasant realities of treatment, you will appreciate my straightforward approach to my narrative. I do not obfuscate my experiences. They are raw, honest, and don't lend themselves to a pretty story, but it is one that needs to be told. I learned coping mechanisms and ways to manage long-term side effects

Cancer. A Journey of a Thousand Miles.

through months and years of trial and error. As I walked my journey, I had very few resources to help me through my struggles. In
your hands is the story of how I made it through the difficult diagnosis, its treatments, AND the stark battlefield I was left with when
the treatments ended. In addition, I hope to shed some light on the following misconceptions.

- Post-treatment survivors aren't immediately "healthy."

- Once in remission or considered "cured," side effects
  promptly disappear.

- Depression and anxiety won't continue beyond the disease state.

- Pre-cancer energy returns to the survivor quickly.

- Social settings are the best way to get back to normal.

- You're lucky if you get one of the "*GOOD*" cancers.

- Everyone is born with cancer cells in their body.

- When it is over, it's over.

This is my story ... my journey through life, cancer, and the
lessons throughout. I begin by introducing you to a younger me
so you can get a feel for who I was as a mature woman when I
received the news. The woman I had evolved into is the one who
pushed forward to slay. And slay, I did.

Chapter 1

THE GROWTH EXPERIMENT

A s the oldest of four girls, I had a good childhood and it was fun watching my three younger sisters grow up. Our parents were loving and supportive; regretfully, I admit, I was not an ideal daughter. I beat up my younger sisters, lied, and stole money from the middle sister (Annie, so sweet and trusting). The hateful gene must've been given to me. Additionally, my academic performance in my senior year of high school fell short, with a "B." Despite my horrid shortcomings, our parents always seemed proud and encouraged me to tell the truth, work hard, set a good example, and strive to reach my full potential.

During my teenage years, I possessed the stereotypical characteristics of a dork: ugly, pronounced overbite, thick glasses, a lack of confidence, and an abundance of shyness and awkwardness. Academically, I found school to be relatively effortless, which, combined with my subdued temperament and nerdy demeanor, occasionally resulted in me being labeled the "teacher's pet." I was fond of math and science (especially the laboratory experiments), playing whiffle ball, running, and being the undisputed neighborhood Red Rover champ. My tenacity was likely the reason behind my unyielding grip during the game. I was so stubborn when there was competition. In general, I was pleasant but challenging to get to know. I was clever but lacked ambition. I wasn't athletic and envied those girls who were. I would have liked to rappel down the gymnasium wall, but fear held me back. I wanted to be a star basketball player but was too passive. I would have liked to have been on the cross-country track team, but I didn't even try out, despite the coach giving me positive feedback by telling me, "I had a good pace." I was excelling, and I was falling flat at the same time—a bundle of chaos and uncertainty. I was a hot mess before the notion of being a "hot mess" was a thing.

I, in a sense, became my own experiment. Big dreams and aspirations filled my head. I envisioned my adult self as a scientist, an astronaut, AND a teacher. However, lofty dreams without action are empty thoughts. There was so much potential harbored within me that was left untapped. It was safe there. Comfortable. By not taking risks, I shielded myself from possible failure. Consequently, any praise bestowed upon me by my parents, teachers, or anyone in an authoritative position was appreciated and adored.

Mom and Dad entrusted the neighboring family to take us girls to church, and I didn't mind it much because I felt a sense of belonging. The Sunday school teachers were terrific and made the learning experience fun. The church was majestic and beautiful and had an adult choir plus a youth choir. Eventually, Mr. Grundy, the choir director, convinced several of us kids to participate in the teen choir, although I couldn't carry a tune to save my life. That still holds today. In December, the towering and baby-faced Mr. Grundy asked the choir members, who were high school band members, to play Christmas music for the remaining (singing) members as we formed a little caroling group. As the group strolled from house to house, some sang carols, and others provided music. It was quite lovely. Mr. G had heard me sing and put me in the little band instead of the choral group; I felt a bit ashamed. Putting the shame aside, I played the clarinet and did it well. Oddly, it was fun - mainly because I didn't have to sing. People were delighted when they heard us, and that brought me happiness. I turned that moment of shame into a more honorable moment. It took each kid in that group to make a joyful noise in the neighborhoods—all of us. Unbeknownst to me at the time, I was developing a nature to serve.

Following high school, I enrolled in college. At that time, I was interested in business. I wanted to avoid an extended academic journey of four more years, so I opted for secretarial studies and completed a one-year program that awarded me a "Certificate of Applied Science." And just like that, college was done.

Daddy

In his younger years, my father served in the U.S. Air Force. He had a tall and slender frame, deep dimples, and prominent cheekbones. His name was Steve, and he was strikingly handsome. Following his military service, he found employment at Owens-Illinois, a glass bottling and manufacturing plant. He held various positions within the company, including in corrugating, plastishield, and bottling. He worked rotating shifts, making it quite a challenge for my giggling (or squabbling) sisters and me to keep quiet when he slept during the day. Dad, a determined and strong-willed individual of Belorussian descent, had a predictable temper, but his sense of humor was unrivaled. He was astute and insightful. Although he hadn't obtained a high school diploma, he later pursued and completed the GED test in his late thirties or early forties, which rightfully brought him a sense of accomplishment. I couldn't have been prouder of him!

Dad had a talent for drawing and created the most interesting and comical cartoon characters. He drew them in a spiral notebook, which was stored away in a musty and yellowed box. The box was like a treasure trove for my curious mind. It contained photos he took from the Korean War, ribbons from his uniform, postcards to my grandma (his mother), a notebook of electrical gibberish I didn't understand, and the drawings. I admired my daddy and tried to copy his illustrations, but it came naturally to him and not to me. He was an outdoorsman with an insatiable desire to be hunting or fishing. He

ME AND MY DADDY

often went on hunting or fishing trips, but that never encroached on his time with the family.

Daddy was the best, and we always got to go on a vacation somewhere. They weren't extravagant, but we didn't know that. We were having fun wherever we were. Camping and fishing in Romney, WV? Perfect! Disney World? Sure, who wouldn't want to go to Disney? Goofy was my favorite! Visit our aunt and Uncle in Tampa? Let's go! I remember picking fresh oranges off the tree and trying my first mango and papaya there! Ocean City with our cousins? Great! There, I had my first taste of beer, even if it was just the little bit left in the bottom of Dad's can of Michelob Light. I sat outside our room on the bay in a weathered Adirondack chair, basking in the sunshine, slowly sipping that quarter can of warm beer, pretending to be a seasoned beer drinker. However, in reality, I probably just appeared like a dorky little girl clumsily pretending to be a grown-up in a somewhat awkward and comical way.

I'm thankful that social media wasn't around then! <<sigh>> I'm sure YouTube would've been blowing up with views of this bony little girl with stringy hair and a mouthful of metal on her prominent overbite, sitting proud as a peacock pretending to have been drinking all afternoon. If mortification had a number, that would've been a ten out of ten.

Family time was the best. Being a daddy's girl, I relished the moments spent fishing alongside him, eagerly assisting with whatever tasks he entrusted me. His approval meant the world to me. The last fishing trip we shared took place in October of 1978. It was an overcast day, accompanied by biting cold winds that stung my face and left my skinny little hands frozen to the bone. Naturally, the murky Tygart River produced <u>no</u> fish for me, but my dad caught <u>a bunch</u>. He found amusement in my shivering and complaints about the snow coming our way. It simply didn't seem "normal". So, tell me, normal people don't usually fish when it's snowing, do they?

Shortly before my twenty-third birthday, just an hour before I was to go to work, my cousin called, telling me to meet her at my parents' house. My heart raced, and a feeling of sickness consumed me. Instinctively, I sensed that something was wrong. I mean, it was 6:30 a.m. Sweating profusely and out of breath, I burst through the front door of my parent's house to find my cousin Jenny on her knees before my mother, both in tears. Jenny held my mother's hands tightly. I stood there in utter horror, my gaze fixed on Jenny, desperately waiting for an explanation. With a trembling voice and tear-filled eyes, she stood and softly spoke the devastating truth, "Your dad didn't come home from hunting yesterday. He was shot and killed."

Numb. I was numb. And I was lost. And scared. He was fifty-three. What were we going to do?!

The Department of Natural Resources, County Sheriff's Office, and State Police had initiated a joint search in the woods near where Dad parked his truck. The property owner noticed his vehicle was still parked there and notified the authorities.

Helicopters flew overhead, with large spotlights cutting through the foggy spring air, and the officers brought in search dogs. They eventually found him. He had been shot in the back of the head while calling turkeys, sitting beneath a tree. My daddy was gone. Like a vapor. Gone. On May 2, 1983, my heart shattered, and I, as a girl, had to try to pick up those shattered pieces and grow into the shell of a woman I was unprepared to become. Time stood still. That was a difficult lesson in strength. Life as I knew it changed forever.

Mom

My mother, Rebecca, was a vision of beauty with her lustrous dark hair and captivating dark eyes. She always dressed elegantly, wearing stylish attire, donning red lipstick, and enveloping herself in the enchanting scent of Chanel No. 5 perfume. Mom, a homemaker, faced partial disability later on and became an example of incredulous strength.

MY MOM AND ME AT EASTER

When I was only five years old, my sister, Annie, was taking a nap while I played on the patio. Amusing myself by blowing the fluffy, floaty things off dandelions, I saw Mom climb the steep cinderblock stairs to feed our beagles.

Moments later, I watched a terrifying incident unfold before my eyes. After she fed the dogs, I watched as she lost her balance and tumbled down those sharp-edged cinderblock stairs.

Miraculously, she landed on the retaining wall, and I vividly recall the mixture of fear and relief that engulfed me when she managed to stop there and not fall onto the patio four feet below. In my memory, the wall appeared to be towering at a height of at least ten feet. I screamed and trembled, though I cannot recall whether she got up on her own, if my father came to her aid, if neighbors rushed to assist, or if I continued to stand there, frozen.

I do remember that my mother had numerous doctor appointments following that incident, some even requiring a nearly four-hour drive to a hospital in Bethesda, MD. While there, doctors performed a biopsy, removing a portion of my mother's left bicep for testing. She went to many appointments. Eventually, she received a devastating diagnosis of Primary Lateral Sclerosis (PLS) — that, coupled with the prognosis, meant that she would require a wheelchair within a decade. The degeneration of brain neurons inevitably meant that her muscle tissue would deteriorate.

It is difficult for me to fathom the emotional impact of hearing those words had on her. PLS was, and remains an extremely rare condition. At that time, she was one of only five known cases in the country. Sadly, there was no specific treatment available for PLS. She became a case for the books, a part of the research. It wouldn't take her life, but it did wear away a part of her spirit. Mom was only in her thirties when this condition attacked her.

Over the next ten years, my mother's condition deteriorated, manifesting as frequent balance issues and progressive muscle loss. She relied on canes for support, specifically the aluminum kind that wrapped around her forearms. As her leg strength diminished, walking for extended periods became increasingly difficult. During my teenage years, our trips to the mall necessitated an adjustment to a wheelchair. My three sisters and I took turns pushing her through the hallways. Through my early adulthood, my mother's decline persisted, noticeable by a slight dragging of her foot while walking. After some time, she transitioned to using a walker for mobility. Despite her difficulties, my father remained steadfastly by her side, taking us on family vacations as if everything was how it used to be. It must have been challenging for him to witness his wife's health steadily decline. As for my mother, the inner torment she must have endured is beyond my imagination. Not once did she utter a complaint, grumble, or express any self-pity. Never! She consistently wore a smile, prepared dinner for our family, took pride in her appearance, and expressed a desire to go out and explore. I often wonder if she silently struggled and, if so, whom she confided in. Why wasn't I more empathetic and understanding? I must've been such a disappointment. I am crying now (in this remembrance).

When my mother reached her fifties, she faced another formidable adversary: breast cancer in her left breast. Thankfully, the doctor caught it early, and she was fortunate enough to avoid chemotherapy. After five weeks of targeted radiotherapy, the cancer was eradicated. Mom had already endured more than her fair share with both PLS and cancer.

However, fate had more in store for her. In the autumn of 2014, five months before her eightieth birthday, she was diagnosed with thymus cancer. Anger surged within me. Hadn't she already faced enough hardships? But, in true characteristic fashion, my mother exemplified poise and grace. After careful consideration, she chose not to pursue further treatments, prioritizing quality of life over quantity.

She succumbed to the illness four months later, in February 2015. Through it all, my mother proved to be the epitome of strength, rising as the most resilient woman I have ever known. Her life had been setting an example for mine, yet I was completely unaware of that.

Yet another lesson of courage, that I didn't want to learn, was punched into my heart.

Chapter 2

A VISION

T wo. I had experienced two significant relationships, both ending in painful breakups. Following those experiences, I decided never to enter another serious relationship or marry. Clearly, I lacked the necessary skills for successful romantic partnerships. However, I found I was comfortable in my skin and was confident that I didn't require a partner to feel complete, and I was finally empowered. In my fifties, I became Wonder Woman. (It was a wonder this woman still had her mind.)

FIRST LOVE

The dissolution of my first relationship was my doing, and I, admittedly, was wrong. I didn't work hard enough to make it work. BJ and I got serious when I was at the tender age of twenty; I now believe I was more in love with the **idea** of being in love than I was in love with him. We were both young. We both had our faults, as everybody does. I, though, was being influenced by a self-absorbed women's "rights" culture that I didn't even understand. That was unfair to him, and I was naively unaware.

In July 1977, I met BJ when I was a waitress at Fairfield's take-out Dairy Desserts ice cream shop. He was a cute twenty-four-year-old salesman at the shoe store just a few blocks away.

After his shift, he would ride his little blue Suzuki motorcycle to where I was working, and he'd order a banana split so that he could see me. He didn't even really want the banana split; it was a choice that would allow him to sit in the parking lot longer. He ordered the same thing every day and threw most of it away every day. It wasn't the ice cream; it was the visit he was interested in. The bike ride was only a few blocks away, but that wasn't important. What mattered was that a boy, rather a "young man," genuinely wanted to see ME. He had the bluest eyes, dark wavy hair, and a freckled face with an ornery grin. And the shirt he had unbuttoned to impress me, did. BJ had a hairy chest and armpits that made my eyes go directly and uncomfortably there when he wore a tank top in the summer. That mass of furriness was a curiosity to me. With my limited dating experience, I found myself fixated on this patch of alpaca fur because my dad didn't have all that under his pits. I wondered, which one was the freak? Probably my dad.

BJ's affection for me grew, and he began mailing me greeting cards. A massive number of cards! Sometimes, they'd arrive daily. I cherished each one, carefully storing them in a Frye boot box hidden under a crocheted blanket — on the top shelf of my closet. We began dating, fell madly in lust, and then rapidly moved to wildly in love.

My life was ideal, and we eventually purchased and moved into a house across the street from his parents. It was a two-story fixer-upper built in the early 1900s with weathered grey

14

paint peeling off the exterior and cable windows in the interior. Despite its worn appearance, we believed it had great potential and saw endless possibilities. We were right. The home was adorned with push-button light switches, hidden pocket doors, a reception room, and the most beautiful oak baseboards and moldings. It was perfect for us.

Just three weeks after settling into our abode, I became pregnant. BJ and I were overjoyed. If the truth be known, we were both most likely grappling with a certain amount of fear and apprehension — I know I was. In May 1981, we instantly transformed from a couple into a family. Nine months went by in about nine minutes. Our firstborn son brought us immeasurable joy and was, in our eyes, absolute perfection. Of course. Motherhood agreed with me because I realized I had a life purpose. Three years later, we welcomed the arrival of a second son, further expanding the love and happiness of our growing little family.

We dedicated ourselves to working on the house whenever our finances allowed. A high school graduate, BJ worked as a vault teller for the Bank of Fairfield in West Virginia. Seeing him leave the house each morning, dressed in a shirt and a tie, filled me with pride. He exuded importance; therefore, he was important. I eagerly sought out a "real" job of my own. Located in my hometown was a large underground coal mine. As fate would have it, the coal company advertised for a clerical position in the local Times. I mustered up the courage to apply and was granted an interview opportunity. Despite my shyness and apprehension,

I marched into the personnel office, pretending to be full of confidence and maturity. I wore a professional yet bohemian and trendy outfit: a long brown jersey knit skirt paired with a cream camisole. The cami was layered with a burnt orange jersey knit jacket that was neatly tied at the waist. On my feet, I donned a pair of alluring Candies wooden-soled platforms to elevate me to almost six feet. I ensured my hair and makeup were impeccably done. I presented myself well, and that likely played a part in securing the job. The Personnel Director conducting the interview happened to be a man. Regardless, I landed the position, which offered a wage of $3.45 per hour. Considering the minimum wage was $2.20, I felt incredibly grateful.

During my tenure at the coal company, I managed to form some friendships, but I struggled with true personal growth. Professionally, I was doing well and eager to learn more. This became a source of tension between BJ and me, as he started to feel resentful because I had consistent promotions and higher incomes. Money continued to be a pressing issue, particularly as our boys entered school. I recalled from my school days that children from families with higher financial means were often considered the "chosen" ones. I wanted my children to have that advantage, so I dedicated my paychecks to dressing them in trendy brands like Lacoste, Air Jordan, and Calvin Klein. I believed that by presenting an appearance of being wealthy, they would be more accepted, regardless of our humble address. However, this prioritization meant that money became tight for secondary expenses such as

16

gasoline, electricity, and medications. My priorities were skewed, and so were BJ's. He admittedly spent more than he should have on baseball cards and collectibles, as that hobby seemed to consume him. Looking back, this perception may not have been entirely accurate, but that is how it felt to me as a young partner of ten years. While he pursued his interests, I found solace in alcohol, feeling increasingly alone. Straight scotch was my drink of choice. Depression took hold of me, and it's unclear which came first or whether one fueled the other. The deeper my depression grew, the more frequently I turned to alcohol as a coping mechanism. While BJ had a circle of baseball buddies and enjoyed his guy time with them, my only semblance of "friends" were my coworkers.

BJ and many others thought I was quite pretty, so he kept tight reins on me when I wasn't working. He demanded to know my whereabouts and what I was doing every minute of every day, and instead of drawing me toward him, it pushed me away. Depression constantly ate at me like a deadly disease. Even when I went to K-Mart to get four items and came home with four things but forgot the TV guide (one of the intended purchases), I had no explanation. I couldn't remember. My brain was a confused jumble of nothingness. I didn't know why. And BJ got angry. "You went after four things. FOUR!" I felt stupid. And I wasn't stupid. But he made me FEEL that way. And I felt crazy because I had no idea why my brain systematically dismantled itself. I now know I was overwhelmed. But, as I confided in my only friends, my work friends, I was "encouraged" and "supported" with comments such as, "You don't have to take that — you FORGOT something for heaven's sake" or "no man would tell ME what to do" or "my man doesn't keep a tight rope on me." And, out of naivety, I fell into a deep dark trap. We should have been talking TO each other instead of ABOUT each other – a concept neither of us was familiar with.

I developed new friendships in the company where I worked, which had over seven hundred employees, primarily men. As I matured into a more attractive young woman, I received attention. I certainly didn't feel very beautiful. I felt awkward and ugly.

At first, when these men began flirting, it scared me, and I was repulsed by it. Most of these men had wives. And I had a significant other! I couldn't help but question what was wrong with them. Did they look at their wife like they were looking at me?! Didn't they love them? I remember one incident vividly: just after I entered Chad's office, he started at my feet, examining me inch by inch, slowly and with roguishness up to my breasts. And back down. That's when I interrupted his visual banquet and made a vicious warning about calling his wife to befriend her. Oh, what delightful conversations we could have! The color drained from his face, I stated my business for entering his office, and I'm sure I heard him call me "bitch" as I walked away. Curiously, I never had a run-in with the audacious pervert again. That conversation empowered me. I had spoken up. I took up for myself. Score one point toward being a grown-up.

Greener Grass

(Content warning: infidelity)

As time passed, BJ and I started to fight more frequently and more intensely. We were careful not to let the boys see or hear us arguing. Ironically, that was not good parenting, as we had hoped. It turned out to be the contrary.

Both BJ and I were unhappy in our relationship. During this time, I started developing a connection with Harry, one of my coworkers. His flirting made me feel valued again after a long time of feeling unloved. Eventually, Harry convinced me to go on a week-long trip to Myrtle Beach with him. Despite me claiming to be with my girlfriends, BJ discovered the truth and confronted me over the phone. I attempted to lie, but I was a terrible liar. Our relationship was over after being together exclusively for each other for thirteen years. I felt conflicted because I knew I had once loved him, but I had reached a point where I had no fight left in me. I left the home to protect our children from being caught in the crossfire. When I left, it was a complete shock to our children. As far as I knew, they had never witnessed us argue before, so the idea of their parents separating was unimaginable to them. I knew that BJ would be willing to co-parent and share custody of the boys to bring them up in the healthiest manner possible. However,

I was never more wrong. BJ resorted to legal measures to limit my access to our boys.

It was the most painful experience to watch our children being subjected to their self-proclaimed "Holy" dad, reading carefully chosen scriptures to condemn their mother's sinful behavior. Suddenly, he was a church-going Saint, and I was rubbish to be scraped off the bottom of a vagrant's shoe. BJ felt overwhelmingly alone, and he seemingly manipulated our boys to "father" him as he went through the grieving process of a breakup. My sons hated me. They felt like they didn't know me. Losing their love and trust devastated me as they were the only things in life that mattered. I took responsibility for doing things in the wrong order regarding the relationship with their dad, but even so, they didn't know the whole story. And they never will. I solemnly vowed to go to my grave, allowing them to blame me so they would not disrespect their father. Although I was at an endpoint where I couldn't stand the man, and the two of us could not have an amicable relationship, he was still their father, and I knew I would cause more resentment and division in my relationship with my boys. I plunged deeper into depression.

During that time, Harry became the only person I could hold onto. The heart of my world had crumbled.

Harry was the epitome of handsomeness, and the man's charm was unparalleled. I continued drinking to drown my depression. He drank with me. Although we had a lot of what I thought was fun, I continued spiraling downhill. In reality, it was

20

synthetic fun. He was a former military man, had a good income, and would amuse himself by dressing me up and promenading me around to all his buddies. I was over thirteen years his junior, and maybe that had some bearing on his bragging rights. He flattered, wined, and dined me. He made me feel special. He made me feel cherished.

In 1995, Harry and I became exclusive, and my sons refused to acknowledge our relationship. Harry built a house for us to begin our lives together, and I cried at the thought of it because something so big and extravagant wasn't what I was used to. I felt undeserving. I was fine living in a fixer-upper. Life was a fairytale for the first few years. Then came some medical problems. I had my gallbladder removed and a total hysterectomy. My thyroid was underactive. I rapidly put on weight, which left me more depressed and lethargic, which led to more weight gain. Harry had several bouts with pancreatitis and developed heart problems.

I cried out to God and began praying because I didn't know what else to do. I prayed for God to come into my life and change me, but I primarily wanted to be remade for my partner. I wanted him to love me like he used to. I quit drinking. Not because I had become a "goody-two-shoes," but because Harry wasn't supposed to be drinking with his heart problems and the medications that he was prescribed. So, after much deliberation, I deduced that if I stopped drinking, then it would be easier for him not to drink while he was "mending." He never did stop. We grew further apart; he became predictably and uncontrollably short-tempered

I wondered if he was depressed. But I'd never seen depression manifest that way, so I wasn't sure. He was anger personified. Life was no longer fun for me or anyone in the household.

Every step taken was on eggshells, and I dare not break one. No matter how I tried to please him, it was never enough. The depression kept me tired. I lost interest in life in general. My fatigue and lack of partnership responsibilities, such as cooking and companionship, kept Harry hostile. Life continued this way for years. In our tenth year, while he was at work, he fell about twelve feet off a piece of equipment. The accident shattered parts of both legs and both feet, and he was incapacitated for four months. It was horrible! I applied for a family medical leave to care for him. He needed me, and I needed to rescue him.

I did as much as my depression-challenged energy level allowed. A conscious effort was made to make the best of a bad situation. I arranged to build a makeshift ramp so his wheelchair had better access over the door jamb into the basement, where he would recover. The little neighbor girls colored pictures for him, and I placed them at eye level so he could easily see them, hoping they'd be a cheerful sight. I took hand towels, painted them with "love notes," and transformed them into bibs or large napkins. We purchased a hospital bed and a bedside potty and had the basement shower modified to make it more accessible for him. There was also a gym downstairs, so we were ready when it was time for physical therapy. I am fully aware that this was all minor stuff, but I hoped these little things would make a difference in the gloomy days ahead. Things were going well, considering.

Being a caregiver isn't easy. As dreadful as it must've been for him, it also taxed me. I took everything to heart, and even though our bond had been strained, I loved him with my whole being. I tried. I honestly tried to do my best. When depression knocks me down, it drains my strength. And I was having the life sucked right out of me. I'm sure it's the same for many others struggling with depression. I slept till 10:00 or 10:30 in the mornings but made him coffee and a delicious breakfast nearly daily. I would carry the meal downstairs to the den on a jelly roll pan (yes, it took a tray that big to get it downstairs in one trip). The day quickly came when Harry told me to go back to work. "I'll be fine," he insisted. "The boy (Jack, his son) is here most of the time — or just down the road working at the Tropical Bar if I need him." Jack had always lived with us. But regardless, I was being told that I wasn't needed there — hurtful words to a tired woman.

In hindsight, there had been a HUGE MISCOMMUNICATION. Because what I heard when Harry said, "I'll be fine," was, "After you're gone, Jack can take over/fill in or pick up the slack." What he meant was, "I'll be fine— just prepare breakfast and dinner before you go to work in the afternoons, make sure the laundry is caught up, then check on me throughout the evening .... and have a good shift." How did I finally come to REALIZE this MISCOMMUNICATION? He purposely and shamelessly made it known that I was a poor caretaker and partner who left him in the basement daily to eat a can of cold beanie weenies from the pantry because I would not be bothered to provide. I had become a perpetual disappointment. I resented that because he was the one to insist that I go back to work! And he had a competent adult son right there who I thought could've/SHOULD'VE picked up the reins. Well, he came to resent me, too. He resented me because he felt like I didn't care. I, seemingly, didn't care that he had no food. He resented that I didn't have the energy or the desire to provide for him. And .... his son and entire family turned on me because I wasn't caring for the family patriarch. Resentment all around. Fingers pointed straight at me, shaking in disgust. All because I couldn't read his mind.

In early 2010, I felt like after all he'd been through with the accident and his (still denied) depression, I thought maybe he just needed some downtime. Some rest, relaxation, and refresh time. Perhaps time away from the humdrum of home would help him escape the depression he denied having. I secretly arranged for a golfing buddy to go with him on a golf trip, which I paid for and presented to him on March 3rd as a birthday "gift certificate." The trip was planned for the last week in April through the first weekend in May, when the weather would likely be ideal. The guys would play at Harry's favorite courses in Myrtle Beach, South Carolina. I prayed for fantastic weather for the trip. Harry and I went shopping for new clothes because I wanted "my man" to look nice. I wanted him to have fun, rejuvenate, and return as the "old Harry" I remembered and loved. Maybe time away would somehow have an impact on our relationship. It did, indeed.

In the early morning of Sunday, the first of May, I hadn't been home from work long when the phone rang. The number wasn't recognizable. Who on earth would be calling at this hour? I answered, and the male voice on the other end informed me that my not-so-loving companion had taken our housekeeper (and the caller's girlfriend) to the beach with him! Harry was sixty-four. The girl was twenty-four. I dialed the hotel room phone number I was given with fingers that shook uncontrollably. She answered. She answered! Not the brightest crayon in the box. "Miss Laura, I swear nothing happened. He wanted it to! But nothing happened." I wanted to puke. Had I believed in karma, this was mine.

Scorched Grass

(Content warning: domestic violence)

Right then, my life changed. I trusted no one. When our framed photo caught my eye, I grabbed it from under the dimly lit lamp on the nightstand. I threw it hard enough to break the crystal frame in the bathroom sink. Then, just for good measure, I smashed it again. I packed a few clothes, took the dogs, and headed south to my sister's house in Fairfield. When Harry got back to our house (no longer a home), he called me and told me to get my ass back up there where it belonged. I did not go right away, but I did go. I had to face him at some point. We fought. He denied everything. I "wanted" to believe him. I "wanted" to consider that the entire relationship wasn't a lie. "Tell me the truth," I pleaded. Again, he denied any wrongdoing. It was all in my head. I was creating circumstances that never happened. I was crazy. The tension was unreal. I hated the thick, dark cloud of gloom that suffocated our once beautiful and cheerful home. I now despised everything about my life.

It was an overcast and gloomy day on December 12th when I moved out of that beautiful house into a quaint little log cabin nine miles away. I had never lived on my own before. I took only my clothes, computer, car, a twin bed with linens, a few groceries, a "backup" coffeemaker, the cookware and utensils I'd recently bought, essential documents, an iron skillet, and a few towels. That's all I had. On my own, I was officially poor. Determined to turn my life around and make that little cabin a charming little haven, I reluctantly began accepting charitable donations of necessities from friends and family members. I shopped at a Goodwill and Dollar store and survived on $35 a week for food. I ate many potatoes. Financially, it was tight, but I knew I could do without any so-called luxuries. Never having been on my own before, I didn't realize the outrageous cost of heating a place with propane. I wore many layers of clothing and placed the hand warmers (which I had purchased as glove inserts when I had to shovel snow) along the sides of my body as I crawled into bed for the night. I could see my breath as I breathed and watched every exhale until I finally fell asleep. I quickly ran out of fuel and was

26

left without any source of warmth. $700 every three to four weeks was more than I could handle, and the rent was paid with a credit card. Stress weighed heavily on me.

Being a relatively new Christian, I felt like I needed some substantial proof of his infidelity. Since I was not in South Carolina to witness the two of them having sex, evidence would likely take a while. I am a hard-headed woman, and I could not/would not be persuaded or influenced before I had proof. I didn't want to wrongly accuse him and end our relationship if I could disprove my gut instinct. Similarly, I wouldn't try to work things out if he did break our exclusivity promise. I remembered hearing him talking on his phone in the woods near our house. Why would someone go to the woods to make a call? Only to hide something, right? He "caught" me looking through his phone once, and after it was forcefully grabbed from my hand, he smashed it on the floor, threatening what would happen if I touched his phone again. He'd break my fingers. Part of me believed him. There were just too many circumstances pointing toward my gut feeling though.

It took me a couple of months to come up with the proof I needed to answer my questions. I took the newfound information and went back to where I used to live. I found him sitting at the kitchen table, enjoying an aromatic and sumptuous breakfast of eggs, home fries, biscuits, and coffee. Must be nice, I thought — he had $35 worth of food in one meal on the table. I sat down at the chair 90° to his left and immediately launched into my accusations. Spewing venom, I gave him the proof. I was angry. I was hurt. And I felt it was justified. "I hate you!" I screamed. He ignored me and grabbed a biscuit. Using my left forearm, I forcefully propelled his breakfast off the table and into the dining room. I stood up to scream, "All I wanted was the TRUTH!! Why did you do this? WHY?" I must have pushed him hard and long enough this time because I got "an answer." In his arrogance and vileness, he expelled the most vulgar words I'd ever heard from that man's mouth.

I swear to you, right then, a demon manifested inside me. I could physically feel it coming from my toes up through my body. I tightly drew both fists and started swinging, sobbing all the while, and screaming, "I hate you." I was a big woman, weighing about 220 at that time. I believed I had a little power behind my punch. But no. He was military. He blocked every single swing. That made me madder. Then, I remembered the right hook. Unexpected. Bam! Contact.

I was arrested, and Harry was the victim. According to the law, he was defending himself. The court ordered me to take 26 weeks of domestic violence classes and to stay away from him. I did both. TWENTY-SIX WEEKS. After completing the course, I petitioned the court — without legal counsel, to have the arrest record expunged. The prosecuting attorney's office had no problem with that dismissal because the officer who took my statement on scene had given a good word for me. I suppose he felt sorry for this woman scorned. My petition was granted. I was relieved and grateful.

28

That was my third dose of developed strength. It was a double dose delivered by forceful (and emotional) blows. I didn't handle it well and crumbled to the floor, where I remained for a long time.

The relationship ended. The grass was not greener; it had been burned as the result of a wildfire fueled by lust.

No Plan For A Man

Like I said, I trusted no one. That trust had been breached. All I desired was a life of peace, and being alone was what I saw for myself, so I tried to keep my mind occupied. On my days off, I spent much of my time in Fairfield with my family and my new-born granddaughter, Eva. With every fiber of my being, I believe that God brought that child into my life to help me through that turbulent and complicated time. Eva, the name, means life. And that's what she was to me. She was life to my soul. That itty-bitty girl carried me through the following year.

One gloomy July day, I needed a dose of family. I hopped in the Hyundai, opened the sunroof, and drove to Fairfield. Along the way, men and women were tending to their yards. The fragrance of fresh-cut grass wafted through the air, and children's laughter was nearly masked by the hum of lawnmowers. About forty-five minutes later, when I pulled into her driveway, I was greeted by Donna with Eva cradled in one arm with her weight supported on her momma's hip. Donna is my bestie, almost daughter-in-law, and momma to my granddaughter. Eva bounced with excitement and squealed with delight through the binky in her mouth. I already knew it was going to be a good day. She was only fourteen months old and we giggled and played in her mother's living room. Eva had (and still has) the purest soul and eyes that shone with love. She was always a joy to be around. As the sun began to peek through the clouds, we moved from the floor to the sofa and I quickly read emails on my phone while Eva lay on the pile of pillows. Donna was nearby in the kitchen fixing her nearly world-famous chicken dip, and I could smell the hot sauce and cream cheese as it heated up. I loved that stuff! In the background, I heard a commercial for the Christian Mingle dating site play on her television. Later in the afternoon, it played a second time.

Donna put Eva down for a nap, and on a whim, I grabbed my cell phone and pulled up the Christian Mingle website to set up a profile. Just like that. No thinking about it. No planning. No long-term goals. It was an impulsive notion. I chose a few photos for the profile, including one of me without makeup, and decided on the username (whizzy-wig) WYSIWYG. **What You See Is What You Get.** My profile *clearly* stated that I was not looking for marriage. I was looking for someone with whom to have thoughtful conversations, or perhaps a dinner and an occasional movie. My email address pretty much said it all – it was: noplanforaman. Yes, I was a little bitter. By signing up, I was really amusing myself.

It wasn't long before a few men indicated an interest in me, but no one stood out as a "really gotta meet him" kind of guy.

30

I chatted online with a couple of gentlemen who seemed nice enough. At least on paper.

One guy was Shane. But then he admitted his name was really Derick—red flag. The guy has an alias? Dude, I'm already done. Then, about a month later, I was nearly reeled in by a scammer from Nigeria posing as a businessman from Texas, but I didn't know that at first. His pseudo-name was Duncan. Duncan seemed interesting. We chatted daily, and I was becoming enamored with his sugary disposition. Communication with Duncan continued through emails, phone calls, texts, and sweet talk, and then out of nowhere... bam! Just as the sun was rising one Saturday morning, I answered the phone. Duncan was in a bind (overseas) and asked how much money I could access immediately. None. I have no cash to float across the pond to you, Sir. Consequently, that was the end of the calls. I reported him to the website administrators and learned that some other women had filed complaints, too. Shut down. Liar. Scammer. Jerk.

I felt stupid for allowing my emotions to be played with. I am smarter than that. I actually cried over that. Stupid! Had I already forgotten what I'd come through? Lesson learned. I did chat with, even met, a few other men after that, but the wall protecting my heart had already been rebuilt. I reminded myself that I couldn't trust any of *them*. The term "good man" was an oxymoron.

From that point forward, I made a mental list of "requirements" that a man would have to meet **IF** I were to get involved with him. Since I had no plan for a man, or a woman for that matter, I was reasonably sure that no one would be able to pass my list of self-imposed credentials. But there is a God. And just in case He had a miracle tucked up His sleeve, I would devise a flawless yet practical list of criteria. You know, in case God needed some help. There were certain things I could bend a little on and other things I would not tolerate. If Joe Schmoe came into the picture, and he got to a point on the list where he "didn't fit the requirements," .... bye-bye.... I'm not getting my heart involved. I'm not wasting his time or mine. The plan was brilliant! If the man is not an authentic Christian, he is gone. If he did not some-what share my political views, he was gone. Suppose he had un-controllable anger issues, gone. If he had an addiction to alcohol, drugs, or pornography, he was gone. Suppose he did not respect his family, gone. The list was long, and the line of men was short. That was okay. That was safe.

I met Paul online in the late summer of 2012. After a few emails, we chatted on the phone. We met in person a few weeks later. He had charisma. He was attractive, had striking blue eyes and light reddish-brownish hair, was/is a cancer survivor, and had a bent back because of multiple back surgeries. Based on initial observations, he seemed kind. Genuinely kind.

I learned that he had been through an enormous ordeal that began with a cyst on his upper back and resulted in five back sur-geries with the implantation of rods. Later, because of a bicycle wreck, the rods snapped. Rods in his neck were fused, and he couldn't straighten his back. And he still smiles, I thought. He seemed nice enough, so I continued to see him. His name wasn't BJ or Harry, so "check" (a good thing). He was outgoing and beautifully intellectual. Nothing came up on his background check. (oh, yes, I did!) As weeks turned into months, I tried to find a strikeout SOMEWHERE on my list. I couldn't. I just couldn't. And, this biggie — there was some immediate emotional connection with him that I had never felt with anyone before. It felt strange, and it made me nervous. But I was biding my time because I knew I would find it. I would find that strikeout. His true colors would show. I'd be patient. In the meantime, however, Paul was a seemingly nice guy to "date."

Remember, I had no desire to marry, so I was guarding my heart VERY well. I did not allow him to hold my hand during our first date. We sat in that dark theater watching the movie "*8*", and his hand inched towards mine. My hand fled from his just like "Thing" Aadams. It was a cat-and-mouse chase of handholding. But I proudly prevailed. We had a second date and a third. I did not let him kiss me for several weeks. I know; I was a prude. But my heart couldn't be broken if it didn't get involved. Right? *Right*! Paul persisted and started to get me to loosen up a bit. He did not live in the same town, so he drove an hour to visit me in Johnson County. We would talk, go to lunch, or see a movie. We took long drives in the country in his little black S2000 convertible, and he showed me points of interest throughout his hometown in Tucker County. He was retired but told me about his job as a satellite controller in Washington, DC. He even took me there on one of our dates. Paul enjoyed driving and talking. However, he talked a lot while driving, and the maximum vehicular speed appeared to be 35 mph. Strangely, I didn't care. He was different. And this man managed to make me laugh. And I made him laugh, too. Was it possible that life might be fun again? I was LAUGHING, not loathing. I was caring, not cringing and looking forward, not lying in my rut. I was beginning to feel alive again.

One sunny fall day, he picked me up in the S2000, and we were headed to Tucker County. We had just driven past the Etam Earth station on Route 72 South, and I had an extraordinary experience that took my breath away.

"Whoa," I solemnly said. And Paul, being excessively concerned, asked, "What's wrong? What happened?"

"I just saw myself without hair."

Chapter 3

☺

WILL YOU MARRY ME TODAY?

P aul fell fast, and he fell hard. In love, that is. On the other hand, I worked hard at NOT falling in love. On the ring finger of my left hand, I wore a custom engraved band that said, "Never again." It was a straightforward reminder that I was never to allow myself to fall in love again.

You're probably familiar with the adage, "If something seems too good to be true, it probably is." I bode my time; I knew it would happen. Some nefarious behavior would rear its ugly head, and I would again ascertain that "all men are alike."
There were "things" beginning to pop up. Not bad things, really, just differences. My introduction to his goats was a bit odd. Who has goats as pets? Who has goats - as pets - IN TOWN? Paul. That's who. Thanks, but no thanks. Call me weird, but I prefer canines. (I like goats now) Later, it was pointed out to me that his property was just outside the city limits. Technicalities. That wasn't our most significant dissimilarity. Food. That was a biggie! From his perspective, the most troubling things about me were: I eat chicken wings, pork, venison, and steaks with blood running into the mashed potatoes. However, the most shocking thing to

me was that he ate virtually nothing I did (no exotic, organic, or ethnic foods — ever). The man didn't eat steak. What man doesn't love steak? And I don't care what he said; cubed steak is NOT STEAK. Furthermore, Paul was not a neat freak. Let's say his home was very casual, relaxed, and unorganized. I struggle with what some people call OCD. With my extensive medical knowledge (joke), I self-diagnosed him with OCD, too. Organizationally Challenged Disorder. If it's not a real disorder, it should be! After some friendly bantering, he fired back that there's medication for "people like you who clean with Q-tips and toothpicks." I quipped, "Well, there's no hope for you." Ha!

It was becoming quite clear that we were incompatible. What a shame because he had many positive traits, and I hadn't found a strikeout on my list yet. But sincerely, the man doesn't like steak! I stuck it out for a while longer to see if that was something I could overcome.

We continued to learn about each other. Dating continued as we took short day trips, quiet picnics, and evening movies and had numerous lengthy late-night phone calls. And, every night, he would call to tuck me in before I fell asleep and pray with me. Wow, that was a refreshing twist on dating. He hadn't known me very long, yet he was sincere enough to pray with me every night. I supposed I should let the steak sin go. <<sigh>>

One night, after praying, he quietly said, "I love you." Don't get me wrong, I liked that he was a godly man. But this "*I love you*" stuff? Already?! Impossible. Did the man not know what love is? I didn't sleep well. I tossed and turned throughout the night. When the new day's sunshine poured over my face, what he said the night before still bothered me. When we had our morning chat, I asked him, "Do you remember what you said to me last night?" I quietly panicked. He replied, "Yes". Silence. Deafening silence.

Eventually, I recovered from that but remained cautious and watched the relationship evolve.

Over time, I continued to feel that my connection with this man was deep and emotional. Something I wasn't familiar with, but probably something that normal, healthy relationships had at their core. It was an enigma. It was fascinating!

During an afternoon walk under the yellow-leafed maple trees in the park, he casually mentioned that I should become his wife. Ummmm, no. Not ready for that. We had known each other for four months. He was disappointed that I wasn't feeling the same way but not dissuaded in the least.

Thus began his quest to win over and conquer. Every day, he'd lightheartedly, albeit eagerly, ask, "Will you marry me today?" The man was adorable.

Despite our differences in goats, food, and housekeeping, we found many shared interests between us. Photography, traveling, photography WHILE traveling, family time, going to see movies, having dinner out occasionally, going for walks .... all types of common ground things.

Although ten years my senior, Paul loved to be on the go. He was constantly going somewhere, and he wanted me by his side. I reveled in that attention. We spent a long weekend in the Big Apple, and I was delighted with childlike awe to have seen New York City. We shopped at Macy's, admired the intricately beautiful Christmas window displays, and stopped to enjoy watching ice skaters at the rink in Rockefeller Center. We toured the National 911 Memorial with its reflecting pools at the site of the Twin Towers. It was a place of respect and remembrance but also a sobering reminder of our country's vulnerability. Times Square was a dazzling display of lights, energy, and the bustle of humanity. We made stops at St. Patrick's Cathedral and lower Manhattan's Battery Park, where we could see the majestic Statue of Liberty. We visited the Empire State Building with its grandeur, Wall Street's mighty bull demanding attention, and Madison Square Garden, where the world's greatest boxers have sparred.

I fell madly and deeply in love – with NYC! And I was blessed to have an enthusiastic tour guide by my side. Doing all this on a weekend was a big deal to a small-town girl.

On another mini-vacation, we toured the beautiful state of Virginia and spent time at Monticello, Colonial Williamsburg, and Virginia Beach. Life was good. And Paul was so good to me. Paul was so good FOR me. We had fun wherever we went. And, all these mini-vacations that we took .... two beds. To this day, no one believes that, but it is true. Prude, I tell you. *With a capital "P."* And, God bless Paul — he respected me in every situation! I had that willpower because I was protecting my heart.

It wasn't long after that when Paul, this time against my will, had purchased an engagement ring. He assured me — absolutely no pressure. "If you want to marry me someday, it's yours. If not, that's okay too. I can return it, and I will respect your decision." I was sure I should turn and run fast without looking back. This was my red flag, and I should RUN. Everything seemingly happened so quickly. Dear Lord, I don't really even know him. Not really. Not like I should before considering a HUSBAND. It scared me to know he was serious about marriage. And it wasn't just a fleeting whim or a phase he was going through.

Weeks passed, and he proposed the question with hope every day, "Will you marry me today?" Grinning, I'd respond, "No.... not yet". He continued to court me and was always the gentleman.

One cold November evening, we stopped by Walmart to pick up a few things. I waited in the car to stay warm. My heart began pounding hard, and I experienced this intense itching. When I glanced in the visor mirror, I noticed hives running down my neck and chest—rapid breathing. My extremities became like pins and needles.

Oh. My. Goodness. NO! NOOOO! This was not supposed to happen! At that moment, I realized all the walls around my heart had crumbled. I couldn't stop it if I had tried. My fortress was no more.

It was a relatively quiet ride over the country roads to the little green house with white shutters where he lived. I wasn't very talkative. Shortly after arriving, Paul lit the fireplace, and I changed into my nightclothes, scrubbed my face, and prepared for bed. I heard his happy-self coming down the hallway towards the bathroom. "You okay? What can I get you?"

As I turned toward him with a still-damp face and crazy hair pinned at the top of my head, he could see it in my eyes. I wouldn't say the words. I just wouldn't. If I said it, I had failed my firm resolve.

"I know you do," he quipped with a bit of pride, an ornery grin, and a gleam in his eye. "Just admit it."

Without saying a word, I nodded. There. I gave my confession of guilt. "Happy now? You won." (No. Actually, I WON. This man made me happy.)

By that point, I was ugly crying with mixed emotions and relief. Lots of relief. I was going to be okay. God had my back, and so did Paul.

With a triumphant grin, he asked, "Will you marry me now?"

"Ahh, No. Not yet, I've got to wrap my head around all this".

Undeserving, I was rewarded with a long hug that I did not want to let go of.

Chapter 4

YOU HAVE CANCER

The end of the year was nearing, and I was "at that age", and it was recommended that I have a colonoscopy screening. I'm sure no one ever gets in a hurry to have that done, but I wanted to have mine before the end of the year so I wouldn't have a considerable insurance deductible to start the new year. I landed an appointment for December 31st.

I started things earlier than recommended because I wanted the arduous prep over as soon as possible. The surgeon recommended a Dulcolax/MiraLAX prep, in which four 5 mg Dulcolax tablets were initially taken, followed by a container of MiraLAX mixed with Gatorade. The evening before, I dumped three twenty-ounce bottles of Gatorade into a large pitcher, added the laxative, and stirred till mixed well. Using a funnel, it was carefully poured back into the Gatorade bottles, and I labeled each one and returned them to the refrigerator until morning. Around 11:00 a.m. on the 30th, I took the four laxative tablets. In the next hour, I began drinking and drinking and DRINKING .... until all the mixture was gone. The taste wasn't bad; it mostly tasted like plain Gatorade. Then, off to the bathroom, I went. I sat there, waiting for the dreaded action to start. Nothing happened for the longest time. When things began to move along (pun intended), I was in the poop closet for the remainder of the day and part of the night. Thankfully, I stayed at Paul's that night, and he gave me the bedroom closest to the only bathroom in his humble house. I flushed the last of 2012 down the proverbial toilet. The prep wasn't horrible; it was far from what I'd call desirable, but not horrific. As he drove me to the hospital in Johnson County early the next morning, I was raw, bleeding, and still "leaking." Incredibly embarrassing. My surgeon and the OR staff were fantastic, and one nurse with kind eyes and a gentle spirit quickly assured me that the "leaking" was completely normal and that "everyone has it." Paul remained by my side until a nurse came to wheel me away towards the operating room. He quickly kissed my forehead, said a little prayer, and assured me he'd be waiting for me when I woke. That warmed my heart. It smiled. My face smiled, too. Even though it was weary from exhaustion, it smiled.

Upon waking, I saw that Paul was there as he said he would be, and I learned there were no complications from the procedure. The surgeon told me that she had removed several small polyps and didn't seem concerned. No concern from her translates to let's get the heck out of here because I need an industrial-sized coffee, STAT.

The following day, Tuesday, January 1st, 2013, Paul brought me some piping hot coffee with a generous splash of hazelnut creamer. He turned on the fireplace to rid us of the night's chill, reached for the TV remote to turn on the news, turned toward me and casually asked, "Will you marry me today?"

"Yes," I replied, trying to be relaxed.

I'm not sure who was more shocked, he or me, upon hearing that fall out of my face. He jumped up to get the ring (before I changed my mind, I suppose), and he slipped that gorgeous diamond on my finger. Could my life be any better?

Seven days later, she sat close to me at my routine follow-up appointment, nearly knee to knee, in Examining Room 2. The surgeon looked deep into my soul as she spoke. "The biopsy results are back". Dr. Ridgely began reading each word slowly so I could digest them, "*sections demonstrate severely dysplastic squamous epithelium consistent with carcinoma—.*" She continued. Still, I heard only a word here and there. Her voice became so faint that I thought she'd faded off. "*The possibility of **invasive**.... cell **carcinoma** ... fragment.... **benign**... noted.... also .... **concurs**".

Taking a prolonged inhale, she said, "It's anal cancer." I sat there. Shaken.

I wondered if I would soon die.

The 8'x8' room was stifling hot, and the air became thick. There was no sound. There was no motion. Where there was beautiful color on the walls moments ago, all that was in front of me was darkness. I could not feel anything. In the distance, I heard gently whispered, "Laura?" Whenever some fragments of light trickled through, I gradually began to hear her again. Comfort washed over me as Dr. Ridgeley continued.

Then, I remembered my vision from a few months before. I had already been given this news. Should I have been prepared to some extent? I listened. She explained that it was a squamous cell cancer and that about 90 percent of anal cancers are caused by the HPV (human Papillomavirus). "Really?" I thought, "A virus can cause cancer? Why am I calm? Wait! A virus can cause cancer?!"

She empathetically yet confidently continued, "I am referring you to oncology." Strangely, I did not cry.

I don't remember the drive home, but emotions rained down on me hard when sharing this news with my fiancé of **one week**. This was more than either Paul or I bargained for, and I gave him an out. It was all I knew to do—no strings attached. No hard feelings. I was damaged goods. Not who I was last week and, indeed, not who he fell in love with. I wasn't even sure who I was at that moment.

❝ I was damaged goods. **❞**

He didn't see it that way. He pulled me close and although I wasn't aware of it at the time, he intended to love me through every appointment, test, treatment, scan, and most importantly, every teardrop. Dear God, I didn't deserve him.

Sharing the News

I had to wrap my head around the word "cancer." Altogether, shook because I had no symptoms. Read that again. I had no symptoms. I hadn't been ill over the past few weeks or months; I hadn't felt a lump or bump, no lingering cough, rash, tickle, twitch, tinge of blood, or anything else. But now, I was given a beastly battle to fight out of nowhere. I had to figure out what this dreadful diagnosis would mean for me.

How was I going to tell my family? How will my sons react? They'd already lost their father to cancer. My mother! — how could I tell my mother about this? And my little granddaughter and my sisters? Suddenly, I felt an overwhelming responsibility for everyone in my family. It weighed heavily on my shoulders. Nights were long. And restless. Those sleepless periods were often spent creating a tactical plan to deliver this news to those I loved. I couldn't just lay there surrounded by darkness.

For once, my firm resolve and tenacity were positive forces. It pushed me toward the endpoint, at which time I would call a family meeting. I researched online to find all I could about anal cancer. Most of what I found was on the American Cancer Society's web page. I also read that Farrah Fawcett, arguably the most stunning of all young American actresses in the 70s and 80s, had this same type of cancer. She died. I searched for triumphant stories. I saw none. I decided they just hadn't been written yet. I explored the internet for personal accounts of what the treatments would be like and, again, came up empty. I copied and pasted any statistical data and what I considered to be the most significant medical importance into a Word document. To prevent it from appearing too sterile or journalistic, I highlighted, rephrased, and worked to create a "reader-friendly booklet" of information. I printed a booklet for each immediate family member — seven in total.

Everyone immediately knew something unusual was going on when I called a family meeting. There were two meetings scheduled. The first was held at my mother's little apartment in Fairfield. It was immediate family only: my mom, sister Annie, sister Jeannie and myself. My sister Janie moved to Nashville years ago, and I could not drop an urgent family meeting request on her, expect her to drive eight hours, and arrive intact, waltzing cheerfully into mom's living room without a care in the world. It wouldn't have happened. Janie would have driven to Fairfield with an anticipatory ticking time bomb of the unknown as her traveling companion. Her arrival would be as a war-torn mercenary with large, watery brown eyes and a face of uneasiness. It would all be concealed by an obligatory smile. I couldn't put her through that, so she and I talked by phone just before the meeting at Mom's.

When everyone arrived at the appointed time, they knew me well enough to know that my light-hearted little wisecrack of "just wanted to see ya ... haha ... bye" was a diversionary tactic. Convinced that I had to be poised and with no indications of fear,

I calmly began sharing- slowly, allowing them to digest each sentence.

"I have cancer" (gasps from each one and seemingly in unison). Adding, "But it is very treatable."

I paused and allowed them to absorb it. Everyone had tears welling up and were about to spill down their cheeks. (I recited in my mind; I WILL *NOT* cry. **I. CANNOT. CRY.**) Drawing a long breath, I gently told them it was anal cancer, the rarity of it, and how I would be treated. Each was given their booklet, and we leafed through the information together. I pointed out the highlighted sections, and we looked to each other for support. I believe they were grateful for the info. It saved them from looking it up online and scaring themselves to death with questions of treatment success and morbidity. We ended with my confident assurance that I would be okay. With tearful and long, loving hugs, we departed. Or at least I did. I imagine they had a brief consolation period or a "what the heck just happened?" portion of the meeting that I wasn't privy to. And that was okay. They needed to be able to be real and to take off the brave faces.

Donna's home would be the next meeting place. Donna is my best friend in the whole world. She and my son, Craig, created this beautiful little soul named Eva. Eva was my only grandchild then, and that girl held my heart in her tiny three-year-old hands. After arriving at Donna's house, the invitees entered her living room with even more trepidation than everyone did at Mom's. I found a comfy spot on the floor in front of the couch. Donna sat perpendicular to me. Craig, to her right, and my younger son, Eric, to his right. The men chose to stand. Eva plopped down in my lap, becoming my living, breathing security blanket. I planned to approach things similarly in this meeting, but I could see inquisitiveness regarding the manila envelope beside me. Each of my senses was hyper-aware.

"Please, God, I need You here. I need Your presence in this room. I cannot do this one without You," I prayed silently. This gathering was going to be more challenging. On me. On everyone. Donna lost her mother to cancer a few years back, and there are days that she is still raw with emotion. My sons' father passed away from cancer. There I sat amid three young people who'd already lost one parent to the cancer beast, and I was about to tell them I had been diagnosed. This was going to be a tough one. Gently, I shared the news while handing out the carefully prepared booklets. No one opened them.

Oddly, I don't recall much about my sons' reactions except empty, blank stares. Their lives, like mine, just seemed to spiral into a deep black hole. Donna shed tears, trembling with intense worry. Eva, of course, was alarmed by everyone's reactions, and I held her tightly. Again, although less convincing, the reassurance of "I'll be fine" came from the elephant in the room. I now had to prove it. Exhausted, I was thankful to have survived the day.

I had to wrap my head around the word "cancer." I never heard of anal cancer. Anal cancer? *Really*?! Leave to me to get butt-hole cancer, over-achiever that I am. Stop laughing.

Questions began to take over my mind. How did it get it? Why did I get it? Was it the virus? Was I going to die soon? What would happen to my soon-to-be husband? Dying was not an option! It just wasn't.

Just yesterday, I was the very picture of health, and with one sunrise, I had been handed the monstrosity of a diagnosis that would likely rape me of all dignity and self-esteem. People don't even like to speak the word "anal." People don't like hearing about it or talking about it. So, there I was with cancer AND a stigma.

I needed to take a step back and breathe. I breathed in with intention, and I breathed out fear. FEAR.

What exactly is cancer?

Contrary to what some believe, we aren't born with cancer cells. We are born with "normal" cells with specific functions and a designated life cycle. These cells can potentially become cancer cells if their DNA is damaged. Every day, some cells are "born" while others are dying. For example, red blood cells live the longest at 120 days. White cells only live a few days, while platelets live ten days or less.

So, how do cancer cells start if we start with everything being normal? When DNA within a cell becomes damaged, those cells are now "different" because they divide (as normal cells do), but these cells have uncontrolled division. The normal cells know when to stop replicating and know when to die. They know the life-cycle rules, if you will. Replication makes sure all is normal in our bodies. Cancer cells are unable to do this, however. They cannot control and restrict cell division. The DNA carries instructions within our body. The altered ones "talk" differently; they look different. If only a few exist, our immune system can handle them. And, sometimes, they'll die off on their own. The persistent ones that keep changing and rapidly dividing uncontrollably become problematic. They clump together (they're not normal, so they keep dividing) and form a cluster. Clusters form tumors. These tumors can now be identified as hundreds of types of cancers.

Blood cancers don't usually form tumors. They are abnormal cells that replicate to crowd out normal cells in the blood. There are different types of blood cancers, just as there are different types of tumor cancers.

I am not a physician, but simply someone who has experienced and witnessed cancer's effects. It is my firm belief that cancer begins with trauma at the cellular level. This trauma can stem from the poisons we put into our bodies (preservatives, hormones, pesticides, GMOs, excessive alcohol intake, secondhand cigarette smoke, and so on). Also, factors such as excessive sun exposure, being overweight, certain viruses, and genetics can also increase the likelihood of cancer.

I believe that this trauma can also come from deep emotional wounds in our lives. In my personal experience, I feel that when I couldn't cope with the intense emotional trauma of a breakup, it affected my immune system, and the emotional distress left a lasting impact on my cells. The pain took a toll on me, and my cells started to mutate and divide. Initially, there was one mutation, and then it multiplied rapidly: one became two, four, sixteen, two hundred fifty-six, and so on, accelerating at an alarming rate. The mutated cells became a tumor. They became a malignant mass. An aggressive, tiny, angry mass. This is my hypothesis, and I'll explain.

When I received my diagnosis, it was less than one year after the most agonizing year of my life. I couldn't handle what I had gone through. I wasn't strong enough. My immune system probably couldn't handle the traumatization and rapid replication of mutated cells.

I researched and learned that anal cancer is a squamous cell carcinoma, like skin cancer. People get skin cancers removed all the time, right? I was cautiously optimistic. That is ridiculous, however. *All* cancers can kill. I couldn't minimize one cancer and overestimate the likelihood of fatality of another. Cancer is cancer. The stage, and therefore my prognosis, would be determined by several factors: the size of the tumor (my surgeon said it was

SMALL — approximately a half inch), the tumor's site (the anal/rectal junction), and whether or not cancer had spread to my lymph nodes (that, had yet to be determined).

I was to have another biopsy taken to see if my surgeon could "get it all." If the second biopsied section had no cancer cells on the outside edges of the specimen, then that would mean she got it all. That would also mean that it had not spread. I had that biopsy done the following week. I needed to know what I was dealing with. I waited, seemingly forever, before finding out the results.

On February 7th, I learned that, indeed, she was not able to get it all. My heart sank like the deadweight anchor from a dilapidated ship.

Meeting with my Oncologist

Before fully grasping the situation, I met with my oncologist, Dr. Michael. A tall man with graying hair, thick glasses, kind eyes, and a prominent Irish accent. "Because the cancer displays some aggressive tendencies," he gently said, "I want to schedule you for a PET scan (Positron Emission Tomography)." This would provide the necessary information he needed to determine the stage.

Upon a physical exam, he did not find any enlarged or tender nodes, so he expected that it was NOT in my lymph nodes. "Right now," he said, "we are going forward as if it's Stage I." His eyes never left mine. Stage I meant that the cancer was localized. The treatment plan was mapped out, and I learned that I'd be going through a regimen of both chemo and radiation (Nigro Protocol). Dr. Michael explained that I would be scheduled for 5-1/2 weeks of daily (5 days a week) radiation therapy and two rounds of 2 types of chemotherapy. The first chemo would be an IV push done by their nurse. The second chemo would take place at home for four days (simultaneously) with the first four days of radiation and then again over the very last four days of my radiation. Ugh. Was this really happening?

Following my rounds of chemo, I would be prescribed injections of a drug called Neupogen, a white blood cell stimulator. The thing that sucks about chemo is that not only does it kill cancer cells, but it readily kills healthy cells too. That could leave me immunosuppressed and vulnerable to infections. My head was spinning from information overload. And although exhausted from my consultation with Dr. Michael, I nonetheless felt good about having him as my doctor. He was kind, compassionate, and knowledgeable. He spent hours with me. If I so much as hiccupped in 1972, he wanted to know. Well, he SEEMED to be that detailed. I could see the gears turning in his mind as I answered his questions. I was comforted by knowing that I was in good hands.

When the results of the PET scan came back, I learned that the cancer was traveling to, and was right at, a lymph node. What that meant for me was that I would undergo another procedure.

My oncologist talked to a surgeon at that hospital and asked her to "find" that hot spot and biopsy it. After nearly three hours (it was "normally" a thirty-minute procedure,) she found it and performed a fine needle aspiration at the site. The aspirate was sent to the pathologist.

When that report came back, they could not confirm or rule out the cellular activity within the node because, as can often happen, the specimen wasn't adequate for diagnosis. The node was so tiny.

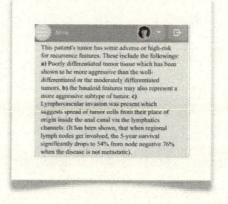

I was staged as a Stage IIIa (I believe precautionarily) because the aggressive and invasive cancer was at the node's edge. My chances of a five-year survival dropped from 76 percent to 54 percent.

Staging

Different components determine the stage. The TNM system is widely used to stage cancer and give the physician a treatment direction.

(T) is the size of the primary <u>tumor</u> in centimeters. One inch is 2.54 centimeters. (The width of a ballpoint pen is about one to 1.25 cm.)

(N) states whether there is lymph <u>node</u> involvement, and (M) indicates if the cancer has spread and how far (<u>metastasis</u>).

	1	2	3	4
T	<= 2cm	>2 - 5cm	>5 cm	spread to other organs

	N0	N1a	N1b	N1c
N	No node involvement	*Lymph node involvement – location and the number of nodes clarify a, b, or c*		

	M0	M1
M	Has <u>not</u> spread	Cancer has spread throughout the body

My diagnosis was Stage IIIA: The tumor was about a half inch in size and had not invaded adjoining organs, but it had spread to a nearby lymph node (abutting it) without spreading to other organs (T1 or T2, N1, M0).

First Things First

The names of my two chemotherapy drugs were Mitomycin and 5-fluorouracil (more commonly, although not affectionately, known as "5-FU"). According to one of the doctors on my oncology team, there was a 60 percent chance that I'd lose most of my hair. Scary words to me. What would I look like bald?

 To become as comfortable as possible with that idea, I tried AND TRIED to convince myself that it's "only hair." I failed miserably. I became terrified at the thought, and I was ashamed to admit it. I played around with digital pictures, removing all my hair. That was my futile attempt to prepare for possible baldness.

Emotions became a struggle that I wasn't prepared for. From deep within, thoughts, fueled by raw emotion, created a violent onslaught within my mind: Baldness. Hair clumps. FREAK. Wigs. Photos. STARES. Pity. Unattractive. Paleness. Dark, hollow eyes. Strangers glancing and then quickly turning away. VOMITING. Weakness and the most terrifying one, ALONENESS. In my heart, I "knew" that I had unconditional support from my fiancé and my family and that they would go the distance with me, but I couldn't make the insecurities go away. The thoughts and words seemed to be screaming at me. It was loud, and it was maddening. At that point, I cried. I cried a lot. And that frustrated me even more because I knew that cancer was becoming more and more common. I wasn't immune. It invades virtually every family, and mine certainly wasn't off-limits.

It is fairly well known now that one out of every three women and one out of two men will likely get some type of cancer in their lifetime. Also, the death rate is about one in five or six.

To me, that is staggering.

I demanded that I not feel any self-pity. I will say that I ultimately succeeded in that, probably because my brain had turned to mashed potatoes. I had a myriad of emotions. However, self-pity was not one of them. With that came the revelation of strength. But it wasn't my own. Any "strength" that I did have come from God. Of that, I am sure.

Pre-treatment appointments and tests

Oncology psychiatric evaluation

When I met the oncology psychiatrist, he asked me many questions. As I answered them, I realized where he was headed. I assured him that I was okay. Physically, I may not be so great, but emotionally, I was fine, considering. Then he said, "I'm going to write you a script, and I want you to fill it because you may not think you need an antidepressant now, but you will." He continued, "You have a lot going on right now. You're working full-time, working part-time with photography, and cancer was just added to your plate. That's like another full-time job." I thanked him, ruminated on his words, and later filled the prescription for Zoloft.

As it turned out, he was right. I went through a wide range of emotions and started to acknowledge that I often struggled to cope as well as I thought I should. I'm human, after all. <<big sigh>>

MUGA Scan

MUGA stands for multi-gated acquisition. Other names for this test are nuclear heart scan (injected with a radioactive isotope), cardiac blood pooling imaging, and radionuclide ventriculography (because it scans the heart's lower chambers — the ventricles).

Some oncologists order an echocardiogram instead of the MUGA scan. This is especially true for patients receiving chemo in the drug class of anthracyclines.

Both chemotherapy drugs that I was given could potentially cause heart problems. Anthracyclines and fluoropyrimidines are both linked to cardiotoxicity. Cardiotoxicity can present one year to twenty years later. Both of my chemotherapy drugs note cardio problems as a risk. Even though it seems like a double-whammy, this is not a common side-effect, but rather a RARE, although serious side effect. If you have multiple cardiac risk factors and non-cardiac risk factors, the risk of it is increased.

Cardiac risk factors include **hypertension**, diabetes mellitus, **dyslipidemia**, smoking, **obesity**, peripheral vascular disease, and an **inactive lifestyle.** (Those in bold were my risk factors)

Noncardiac risk factors include **thyroid disorder**, electrolyte abnormalities, chronic kidney disease, significantly under or overweight, and possibly malnutrition (especially Vitamin E deficiency). Prior heart disease (including a borderline low ejection fraction (50-55%) on this MUGA Scan, is likely to increase the risk for cardiotoxicity.

On the test day, I couldn't eat or drink for several hours prior. I reported to the nuclear imaging department, was whisked away to what I deemed as "the vault," and was injected with a small amount of a radioactive tracer. The syringe was contained in a stainless-steel sheath. That made me wonder how "dangerous" the isotope was — the nuclear medical technologist required that much protection and precautionary measure, yet it's intentionally being injected into me. The young tech's name was Deren, and I remember him being friendly yet very focused.

Deren led me to the testing room, where I was instructed to lie on the machine's table. He then hooked me up with several EKG-like leads.

He carefully explained that the massive camera on the instrument would snap pictures to track the tracer as it pumped through my bloodstream. The test aimed to see how efficiently my ventricles were moving the blood. Anything over 50 percent was considered good. The entire procedure took about five minutes.

There was no pain or discomfort. Afterward, he withdrew the IV and reminded me not to be near children or pregnant women. I was "radioactive." My results were good. Everything was progressing as planned.

PICC Line

Peripherally Inserted Central Catheter (A long tube inserted into your arm that runs through a vein to a more prominent vein near the heart).

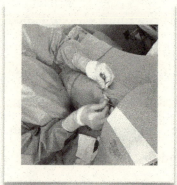

INSERTION OF PICC LINE

The purpose is to provide access for administering medications such as chemo. It can stay in place for months.

This was performed on the second floor, where infusions are done. After being taken to a small, ER-type room, the busyness began with a handful of medical personnel introducing themselves. I was allowed to have someone with me (friend, family).

Not long after, I was asked to lie down on a bed, and they draped me in a sterile paper gown. My right arm was extended to approximately a 90° angle from my body. The arm was surrounded with sterile paper as well. I wore a mask (way before masks were "mandated"). Everyone in the room was required to wear one. An ultrasound was used to find a satisfactory vein, and they bathed the only exposed part of my inner bicep with an iodine-based solution. A numbing agent was used. Wide-eyed, I watched everything, taking it all in. Unaware that a tear rolled down my cheek, I felt Donna gently wipe it away. Gosh, I love her. The technologist told me he was about to begin and said I could look at my vein pulsing in the monitor. It was a robust little thumper. He made a small incision, fished the tube through the vein, and carefully observed the screen as it progressed toward my heart. Donna squeezed my hand, whispering, "I love you," and tears flowed freely.

When the placement had been completed, two access "pigtails" were hanging out of my arm. There were two in case one didn't work for some reason. He slid a partial sleeve of "fishnet" over my upper arm to cover the dangling access lines.

Later in the day, the point of entry became sore. And that was to be expected. Tylenol rescued me. Paul took me home, tucked me into bed, kissed my forehead, and waited in my living room until I awoke from my three-hour nap.

To maintain the integrity of the lines, I flushed them with heparin once a day. A home health agency provided the heparin syringes.

Cancer. A Journey of a Thousand Miles.

Meeting the radiology oncologist

At my next appointment, I was whisked away to meet another member of my oncology team, the radiology oncologist. Onco-radiology was located in the basement of the building. It was eerily quiet and cold down there. Morgue-like, I imagined. Voices seemed to echo through the hallway, interrupting the hollowness of my footsteps. The atmosphere was utterly different upon entering the department. The staff was gracious and welcoming. Dr. Yoon was a talkative one. He handed me the information packet, and I assured him I'd read it from cover to cover. He went over the highlights and introduced me to other staff members. They instructed me on what to expect and what clothing to wear during radiotherapy treatments. Since I was going to have pelvic radiation, it was essential to have my body positioned in the same way each time. I had a photo taken; they tattooed each hip with a dot and made a mold of my legs to ensure I couldn't

 move them while radiating. Nan, one of the radiology techs, reached into a cabinet and brought a pale blue bean-bag-looking thing. I stretched out on the table and put my legs on the bean bag. "If that's uncomfortable, wiggle around until you find the most comfortable spot. You're going to be in this same position every day for 5-1/2 weeks," Nan gently said. I gave

my approval, and they suctioned all the air from the bean bag (it wasn't beans; it was a foam substance).

When I finished as their patient, they removed the plug, allowing air to reenter and making the mold squishy. After sterilization, the mold would be ready for the next new patient (who would be starting radiation) to use.

Chapter 5

GOING VIRAL

A nal cancer was, and still is, considered "rare." The American Cancer Society estimated that in 2013 (the year I was diagnosed), there would be about seven thousand new cases. I was one of those. They also estimated that there would be about nine hundred deaths (two-thirds of those would be women). I didn't want to be one of those.

In 2024, the statistics predict the number of new cases is expected to be over ten thousand five hundred, with about a 2:1 ratio of women to men. The data suggests that there will be nearly two thousand two hundred deaths, with the majority of those (54 percent) being female.

Am I the only one who is outraged? Eleven years later, the death rate has INCREASED by approximately 143 percent! We must get it together and **TALK** about this cancer. Not only screening tests and colonoscopies but also symptoms to watch out for. We aren't catching it early enough.

As previously mentioned, I learned that nearly everyone has had some HPV (Human Papilloma Virus), but there's no way to determine what subtype(s) we might get.

Those who know me well know that I educate myself when I have questions.

65

About forty-two million Americans are currently infected with some type of HPV. That's mind-boggling! And that number increases by millions each year.

HPV was named "human papillomavirus" because a papilloma is a benign wart-like growth, and some HP viruses cause warts.

Plantar warts (those seed-like painful things commonly found on feet) are caused by HPV 1, 2, 4, 60, or 63. There's more; two other subtypes cause genital warts. Even though symptoms can be as benign as warts, most people never have any symptoms, and the

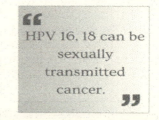

body usually clears the virus on its own within two years.

But the thing is, there are one hundred fifty to two hundred subtypes of HPV, and fourteen of those can potentially cause cancer. HPV causes thirty-seven thousand cancer cases per year. Fortunately, 90 percent of those will be cleared from the body on its own.

The two main cancer-causing types are HPV 16 & HPV 18. Contagious? Yes. HPV is passed from person to person.

The contact doesn't have to be through intercourse, and it doesn't even have to be sexual. With that being said, though, HPV is still the most common sexually transmitted infection in the United States.

Even if you had sex with a single partner in your life, using condoms every time, there is still an 80 percent chance you will acquire an HPV in your lifetime. It's a pesky little virus. HPV can be spread by contact between the genitals and skin, so all people (in any identifying community) can get the virus. It does not discriminate.

The virus can be passed through sex, but it can also be transmitted from:

- mother to child during pregnancy;
- genitals to hands/mouth OR hands/mouth to genitals;
- blood transmission.

There IS A VACCINE available for the cancer-related subtypes. The vaccine is given in a series of two or three doses (age dependent) over six months and is recommended for ages nine-forty-five.

At this time, there's no cure, and there aren't currently any blood tests to confirm HPV status.

Other information regarding HPV transmission and anal cancer:

Congrats. You get a Stigma, too.

Although condoms don't wholly protect, they do help. In general, condoms are 80% percent effective when used 100 percent of the time. And remember, having multiple sex partners not only increases the risk of this cancer, it increases the likelihood of HIV.

1. It's not fully understood why, but uncircumcised men are more likely to be infected with HPV.

2. Here's something else that I found peculiar, if a woman has had some "female" cancer, her likelihood of developing anal cancer increases. This is because those cancers are usually caused by HPVs, too. But men who develop penile cancer (also usually caused by HPV) do not necessarily have an increased risk of anal cancer. Strange huh?

3. Smokers have a higher risk of anal cancer. I want to ask, "Why?" Do toxins in the cigarettes keep mutated cells readily dividing? Does smoking inhibit our immune system from healing our body? Or is mortality affected by the additional risk of other cancers?

4. It's more common in women than men. Unless you're an African-American, then it's more prevalent in men.

5. Again, I don't understand the "why?" Lack of education or healthcare in some communities? No advocacy for early detection? Personal pride (unwilling to talk about it with a friend or physician)?

6. Participation in anal sex increases risk. The virus can be inactive for years and become active for seemingly no reason. I do not know, but sometimes I wonder, if I did have HPV, was it because of something I did or didn't do?

The questions haunted me for years. I was judge and jury for the immature and reckless me, and a thundering voice from within me demanded accountability.

Have I had more than one sexual partner over the years? And my weary- self weakly replied, *"Yes."*

Did I ever have anal sex?
Tearfully, *"Yes."*

Have I ever had sex with an uncircumcised man?
"No."

Have I participated in sex without a condom?
"Yes. Just stop this!!"

Did I receive the vaccine?

Sobbing, "*No. But it wasn't available back in the day!!! Leave me alone!*"

The internal argument was neither productive, nor beneficial. It added to my stress level, and that is all it did. Perhaps I should start drinking again? No. Well, maybe.

NO. Alcohol was never the solution to anything.

I'm not saying that HPV causes all anal cancer, but it is the cause for the majority of cases, and I would rather blame a virus than bear this burden of guilt.

How does this HPV work? Most viruses don't cause cancer, so what's so special about this one?

The HPV takes over normal, healthy cells and interjects its own DNA into them. Replication of those cells begins and continues with mutated DNA. The previously healthy cells can become cancerous, and tumors start forming.

Risk factors for getting the virus can be decreased, but it's not entirely preventable It's a virus. Again, nearly every sexually active person will get HPV at some point in their life and there aren't any blood tests to determine general "HPV status." HPV tests are available to women with their Pap tests — to screen for cervical cancer. Many gynecologists routinely request this to be a "reflex" test for their female patients' annual PAP screenings, if abnormal cells are found. Women need to be proactive about this testing. Please don't be afraid to advocate for yourself and talk with your PCP or OB/GYN about the HPV screening. Ask questions.

I was so paranoid about transmitting this virus to my husband! Again, I was never told I had HPV, but what if I did? Could it still be in my system? Should I not be having sex? He could get penile cancer if he contracted HPV from me. Or oropharyngeal cancer! I could've been a walking STD! The thought disgusted me; I wanted to shower in bleach. Or was I more of a walking cancer cell vending machine? "C'mon, babe — let's see if you get pleasured today or get cancer." I didn't know what to do. I fretted. I cried. I ordered some coochie condoms. A thin film of protective non-latex squares that I thought I could put "down there" if that's the only way we could . . . you know.

I suppose I should clarify. They weren't really called coochie condoms. They were dental dams. But I didn't see why they couldn't be used like that. <<sigh>> And you know what? And they (help) prevent STD transmission. Maybe I wasn't so crazy after all!

So, after talking to my gynecologist, he assured me I was "safe." While I was nearly in tears, I am confident he held back a giggle at my naiveté. Ugh. Men!

Some patients won't even say the word "anal". Others, upon learning the diagnosis, make the presumption that the patient MUST have had anal sex all the time. So, they're a freak in that regard, too. Some patients tell their family/friends that they've been diagnosed with stomach, colon, or even rectal cancer. Anything other than ANAL cancer.

I don't understand this stigma. If there's a body part available, cancer cells can congregate there. We have a brain. Cancer can infiltrate the brain. We have eyes. Yes, there is ocular cancer. Stomach. Yep, mutant cells can live there too. Liver, pancreas, kidneys, gall bladder, mouth, bone, bladder, colon, skin, breasts, prostate, bloodstream, thyroid, rectum, thymus, lungs, and. . . (although rare) the heart. Oh, even the anus. Say it with me now. Out loud. "Anus".

Oh, you can do better than that.

Louder, please.

Let's try that again.

"ANUS! **ANUS!!** **ANUS!!"**

That's right.

Each and every **BODY** has one, so *everybody* has one.

Basically, if a body part is available, cancer cells can replicate there. There is no shame. It's simply a matter of anatomy and replication.

Incidentally, HPV isn't the only virus capable of causing cancer.

These viruses have been linked to the following cancers.[1]

Virus	***Cancer***
Epstein-Barr	*Nasopharyngeal* *Lymphomas* *Stomach cancer*
Hepatitis B/C	*Liver cancer* *non-Hodgkin* *lymphoma*
HIV	*Kaposi sarcoma* *Cervical cancer* *Anal cancer* *non-Hodgkin lymphoma* *Hodgkin disease* *Lung cancer* *Mouth/throat cancer* *some Skin cancers* *Liver cancer*
Human Herpes Virus 8	*Kaposi sarcoma*
Human T-lymphotropic Virus-1	*Adult T-cell leukemia*
Merkel cell polyomavirus	*Merkel cell* *Carcinoma*

---

1.   Wessel, Megan, Wyant, Tracy, Pena, Christopher, et al. "Viruses That Can Lead To Cancer." *www.cancer.org/cancer/risk-prevention/infections/infections-that-can-lead-to-cancer/viruses.html*, March 23, 2023. Accessed 14 Feb 2024.

Cancer. A Journey of a Thousand Miles.

A virus is also being discussed as a possible link to certain cancers in lab animals. However, this has not been proven to be the case in humans, so I did not include that here.

You may wonder why I went into such detail and research to share the clinical aspects of viruses linked to cancer. Simply put, I wanted to understand it for myself. If there was one virus, I imagined there would be more. The burden of expectation began to weigh on my shoulders. I took the responsibility to share my story and educate others.

Chapter 6

BREAKING THE
FINANCIAL CHAINS

M oney. We never seem to have enough. Most people live at or above their means. Most don't think about critical illnesses daily or <u>plan</u> for them. But then, coming to the point of diagnosis, treating, and monitoring the disease process is very expensive and challenging in so many ways.

Insurance

I don't believe in luck, but if I did, I would've considered my turn of events a pot of gold. The year before my diagnosis, the company I worked for switched healthcare plans. Representatives from the new company came in to offer insight into the changes and to answer any questions employees may've had. Working the afternoon shift made things a bit more complicated because the presentations were done earlier in the day.

Carlos was a handsome young man in his thirties. He agreed to meet with our team at 5 p.m. at the round table in the lunchroom. My coworkers and I hoped Carlos wouldn't talk too long because work took precedence over everything, even breathing. Fortunately, the health plans were very similar to what we had previously. But then, we were told about cancer insurance. I'd never heard of such a thing. Cancer wasn't predominantly raging through either side of my family, but my mom did have a bout of breast cancer when she was in her early fifties. "Sure. Sign me up," I said. It was about $20 a month. What the heck? It was only $20 out of my check; it wouldn't be too much of a loss if I never used it.

Little did I know that I would need that supplemental policy to help cover my oncology bills in less than a year. Now, here's the thing: most insurance companies cover cancer. But there are yearly deductibles to be met (I was diagnosed in January), copays, lost wages, medication copays, and so on. Cancer insurance companies will send payouts to you, not the healthcare facility. You disperse it to wherever it's needed. My first check upon diagnosis was for $5,000. That was a blessing. It didn't take but a minute to disperse that. Following the initial payment, I had to keep track of the bills and FAX them to the insurance company. After reviewing and approving, a distribution was made.

If that option hadn't been available to me through my employer, I would still be paying off the oncology bills. That said, if you are disciplined and can put money aside for "what ifs" or "emergencies," then respect to you. <<tipping my hat>> My idea for putting money aside is for vacations, not cancer. But NOW it was real. It can and does happen without warning, whether you have savings or not. It's a common-sense thing, yet most of us don't ponder the possible unpleasantries of life.

My total medical bill charges were astronomical. I had routine follow-up PET/CT scans every six months, follow-up co-lonoscopies every alternating six months, and yearly chest X-rays. Once in a while, an extra test was ordered. Over the years, I paid between $10 and $700 monthly towards the balance. I did miss a month once in a while, which did not make them happy. I did what I could when I could. Eventually, an energetic young girl called to set me up on a payment plan. "Can ya do $100 a month?" she questioned. Exasperated, I bit my lip and slowly told little Miss Vim and Vigor, "No. I cannot. You see, this is not my only bill, nor my only MEDICAL bill". I heard, "Yes, ma'am, I get it." (No, she didn't — she hadn't a clue.) I, now "Miss Vinegar," offered up $25 a month, which was a pittance, but that's what my check-book would allow. Plus, I was tired of Miss Candy-coated Vim and Vigor driving a toothpick into my ear and had to go puke at that moment.

Since it was a significant benefit to me, I strongly recom-mend that you consider cancer or critical illness insurance if it's available. You can weigh it out based on what your regular med-ical insurance will cover, if you have long or short-term disability coverage, and how sick days or PTO (paid time off) work within your company. Even with the insurance coverage payouts, it took me eight years of monthly payments to pay off my indebtedness.

FMLA

The Family Medical Leave Act (FMLA) has allowed many people to care for themselves or a loved one in medical situations where it's necessary to be home. The act will enable you to take up to twelve weeks' leave in one year (if you've been employed there for at least twelve months) while protecting your job seniority and your right to health insurance as your company offers.

Once I had exhausted my PTO (Paid Time Off) hours, I was permitted to petition the other staff at the facility to donate a portion of their PTO surplus hours to me to maintain an income for a while. This is a wonderful plan for most employees as it genuinely benefits them if they are well-liked and sociable. I received enough time to cover me for two additional days.

No Insurance

When the time came for me to retire, I lost my insurance. This was the case for two years. The Affordable Care Act (ACA) was not going to be beneficial for me at all. The monthly payments plus the deductibles were insane. I'm not sure who the ACA is affordable for, but it certainly wasn't me.

In light of that, I made an insane choice. I would not go to the doctor, dentist, eye doctor, oncology follow-ups, etc. Unless it was a true emergency, forget it; I won't go.

Guess who got Covid three times? Guess who grew a cyst that rendered her unable to walk? Guess again as to who.... and it goes on and on. I truly believe that God has a sense of humor. I say, "I'm not going." He says, "Oh, you're gonna go. You NEED to go".

And it continued this way for two years. I waited until I couldn't hold out any longer and then reluctantly resigned to getting help outside myself.

Once again, medical bills piled up. Once again, a little miss Sunshine would call. I paid what I could and left some to sit, and those were eventually turned into collections, and my credit score plummeted. What a pleasure these medical bills were (and are). So, I regrouped and tried to determine where I could pinch pennies. The first thing I cut out was home meal delivery kits. The next thing was not to buy any shoes for a while. I put shoes and clothes that I didn't wear into consignment. I did what I had to do.

Disability

I thought I might qualify, so I applied and was approved for disability. I suppose I should say that I was unfortunate enough to have so many issues that I was approved the first time. There was no reapplying, no hiring an attorney, and no fight whatsoever. Bam. Approval.

The checks have been a welcome supplement and tremendous relief from the financial strain. After a twenty-four-month waiting period, I obtained Medicare parts A and B and a supplemental policy to cover almost any need. I am so grateful for all that it has provided me with. I go to the doctor now when needed.

Chapter 7

WIN SOME.
LOSE SOME.

F riends, that is. Yes, during cancer, we often find out "who our real friends are." It's sad, really. Oh, I received a number of calls, but over time, at the heart of many of those calls was the need to know when I was returning to work. There was talk of filling my position with a new hire. Imagine hearing that when you had just completed treatments weeks before and continued to suffer from profound exhaustion, radiation burns, and radiation-induced enteritis. I begged and pleaded with my oncologist to release me EARLY. I needed my job. I had bills to pay. I had cancer treatments to pay for! Reluctantly, Dr. Michael did give me partial approval, but there were a lot of stipulations. I would be easing back into work life exceptionally slowly. I worked a couple of hours (a couple of days a week) and increased hours as I could tolerate it. I, essentially, put my job ahead of my health. I didn't experience being a valued employee; instead, I felt like a mere "warm" body, expected to perform my duties regardless of illness. My return seemed to be met with indifference from most people. It was almost like they were afraid that they'd "catch" it. There were a few "How are you?" questions and a few

"You look good" comments. I felt like it didn't matter that I had been gone, and it didn't matter that I was back.

The reality was, they were being polite. They acted like they thought they were "<u>supposed</u>" to act. And it's not like I expected some ridiculous cult following; it's just that I was so proud of myself for getting through it! I suppose I hoped that someone would authentically share my excitement. This wasn't a pity party for me; it was simply how it was. There were a few exceptions, and I counted them as real friends. Ted, one of the department supervisors, Dave, Katie, and Mary Lou. They welcomed me and were indeed happy that I was doing as well as I was.

There were lessons to be learned. How might I have responded had I been in their shoes?

I didn't see all this during my fight, but I learned a lot retrospectively, which prompted this chapter. I came to realize why some people reacted the way they did.

Cancer is tough on relationships. I was fortunate to have a strong support system of family and close friends, but many people don't have that. When I was diagnosed, as I'm sure is the case for many others, my focus was on my health and not on how friends would react. Some of my friends, like my friend Robert, went far beyond any expectations that I may unconsciously had. Some people treated me as though I had the plague. Others were painfully indifferent. I learned that this wasn't uncommon. People often don't know what to say, so in fear of saying the "wrong thing," they say nothing. They will disappear. So, they don't have to see you. So they don't have to see **IT**. One thing became apparent: the "fight or flight" principle applied to more than me, the patient.

Idea suggestions to let a survivor know you care

Send a card

For me, cards were very appreciated. They were a tangible sign that I was being thought about and supported. Treatments sucked the life out of me, and I wasn't physically able to talk on the phone day after day, telling the same "how I'm feeling" story repeatedly. Mary Lou and Katie, from work, sent cards several times a week. They were encouraging, and the sentiments often brought me to tears! I also received cards from a couple of people whom I would never have expected to be thinking about me. Those were not only a surprise, but they touched my heart. To know that acquaintances took the time to pray for me and to send me a card, well … I was overwhelmed with their kindness. Their thoughtfulness meant so much more to me because of the many other superficial friends who gave a patronizing "Hi, how are you doing?". Also, it was nice to read the handwritten sentiments. Seeing the words "I admire your strength as you are fighting this disease" was heartwarming. It meant something and I still have the cards.

Fix a meal (or three)

Another coworker prepared an entire meal and delivered it to my home. Wow. After a busy and exhausting day of treatments, this was a wonderful surprise, and it was not only delicious but also much appreciated. I began to think and expand on that, being convinced that crock pot meals would also be excellent. Freezer meals would be an idea, too. Maybe make a casserole in a disposable dish that can be frozen. The patient (while taking treatments) may not have much of an appetite, but a neighbor, friend, or caregiver could reheat the meal when it's most needed. There's also the meal train. The meal train is an online concept where people (book club, church group, crocheting friends, garden club, etc.) sign up to cover meals over a designated period. The volunteers promptly deliver meals, and there's no work or worry for the patient or caregiver.

Send something handmade

I love giving AND receiving hand-made gifts. Knowing someone took the time out of their busy schedule to make something just for me is fantastic. I received several beautiful surprises that I'll keep forever. I received a teddy bear from a lady at work. The women at my church knitted me a prayer shawl. A dear friend from high school made me a scrapbook for my cancer journey.

All I needed to do was insert photos. I don't know if men would appreciate the scrapbook like I did, but I loved it and wanted to share that idea with you. I have created scrapbooks in the past, and I know how time-consuming the process can be. Nancy gave the gift of thoughtfulness, her time, and creativity.

Put together a chemo care package

Donna, not only held my hand through my first chemo, but she also put together an incredibly thoughtful gift bag, a chemo survival pack. Inside the colorful bag was a fuzzy blanket (because chemo makes you feel cold), teddy bear (always someone to hug), a paperback book (a nice distraction to help pass the time), lotion (for dry skin), whimsical socks (a fun way to keep my piggies warm), ginger tea (for an upset tummy), hard candies (for a sore mouth), tissues (to dry any tears), flavored toothpaste (if I developed the metallic taste in my mouth — and I did) and a framed photo of my beautiful granddaughter (to make me smile). Chemo survival packs don't have to be extravagant. Genuine thoughtfulness will make such a difference in a patient's day.

Just keep in touch.

Cancer is not a contagious airborne infection. You won't catch it by being in the same room. It's okay to tell the patient, your friend, or family member that you *don't know what to say.* It's okay to listen. It's okay to feel awkward. But keep in touch. Letting the one you care about know that they're being thought about or prayed for can brighten up an otherwise tough day. Be sincere in all that you say or do. Ask <u>when</u> would (not <u>if</u> there would) be an acceptable time to visit. Leave it up to the patient.

Organize an effort to "honor" the survivor.

My sister, Annie, created an awareness project. She made lanyards, key rings, and fobs out of survival cord (get it, 'SUR-VIVE'-al cord). She called her project *"Lolly's Lanyards"* and do-nated them to the cancer center, where I received treatment. Lolly is my nickname, and she had informational scrolls that were given out with each item. It was awesome.

Another thing that could be done, is walk in a Relay For Life event in honor of your friend or family member. You don't have to have a huge team; just walk. Be there as a representative for someone you care about. It's a way to show that you support a survivor.

Whether your friend or loved one is actively fighting or in remission, they are survivors; and that's worth honoring!

Wearing cancer awareness bracelets to show your support is an excellent way to encourage a patient. It is a small, simple gesture, yet meaningful.

Ask how you can help (not "if" you can)

Often, it can be easier for someone to accept help if you offer support. Sometimes, a patient doesn't want to ask for help or burden others. You might offer to drive him/her to an appointment, help with gas money, babysit or dog-sit, ask if you can do some household chores for them, offer to get their mail, pick up groceries/prescriptions, or provide emotional support while wig shopping.

Whatever you do, do it with sincerity and no strings attached.

Organize a benefit

Organizing a benefit can raise money to help with the patient's mountain of medical expenses.

A chicken roast or spaghetti dinner are both excellent fund-raisers. Elimination dinners are always a hit. Some online sites permit you to set up a page for online donations. As I mentioned, corporate employers and smaller occupational businesses may have a program to petition other employees for time donations when the patient/employee has exhausted all their sick or vacation days. This can provide income when benefits run out.

Statements that didn't encourage me
(although they were meant to)

I understand

Please don't say that you understand if you haven't been there. Cancer is a ruthless beast. Chemo and radiation can be torturous. Don't tell me you "get it" if you haven't gone through it.

So and so's experience

I didn't want to know about Uncle Joe, who suffered horribly through chemo, or that Aunt Millie died from the same cancer. I didn't want to know that your sister-in-law was in remission until the cancer spontaneously returned and metastasized. While you may feel like sharing information will help me not feel alone, I found it depressing. I had a demon to face. Please don't discourage me, as I am taking up arms to fight.

"At least it's not..."

"Well, I guess if you have to have cancer, that's a GOOD one to have."

After getting a cancer diagnosis, it's difficult to process what that's going to mean for the patient. Cancer is cancer. It kills. There is no "good" cancer. While I do understand that some cancers are more treatable than others, I was vulnerable and didn't want those with a pretentious tone to ask me to presume everything was cut and dry. Again, all cancer is terrible. Was I hypersensitive? Maybe. Maybe not. I think a lot of men hear this with a diagnosis of prostate cancer because it is believed to be "very treatable."

Insincerity

Please don't say, "Call or text me if you need anything," if you don't indeed mean that. I wanted friends I could count on. I wanted to know that you will be there if you offer. Life can get in the way of "I need you" requests. But most people are wise enough to notice when explanations aren't adding up. Don't pretend. I didn't have the time or energy for deceitful people.

Shush

Please don't tell me to quit complaining, grumble to others that I am moody again, or roll your eyes as I walk away. We all have good days and bad days. Bad days for me were exhausting and overwhelming. Sometimes, I needed to verbalize it. Sometimes I just needed to cry. I know that many people didn't understand. I accepted that. Please don't make things heavier for me to carry by implying that I ruined your day. Lighten up a little and take a step back.

Remember: there's still a lot going on inside

Even when the cancer is GONE, it can take up to two years, or more, to regain the strength we once had. Side effects from radiation and chemo can present up to ten-twenty years later, and the strength-sapping treatments take their toll. I wished people would remember that I was not lazy. I wasn't looking for sympathy. I was depleted of all the strength that I had (physically, mentally, and emotionally). Sometimes, it takes a while to recover fully. I didn't understand all of the post-treatment sequelae myself and became exasperated when I was forced to explain myself to others. I hated the way I felt! It made me bitter to disclose such personal information that would open me up to more vulnerability and ridicule.

Chapter 8

LET'S TALK ABOUT CHEMO

C hemotherapy is the stuff horror dreams are made of. It's a ... Cancer. Cell. Killer.

My chemotherapy drugs were Mitomycin and 5-fluorouracil (commonly known as 5-FU).

It was cold in the infusion center where chemo was given. Donna sat so close to me, letting me know she would always be there. A young man sitting across from me had already lost his hair and eyebrows. He had an empty look, and each time I glanced at him, I wanted to run and not turn back. Despite mustering a faint smile, he appeared to be wrestling with a sense of defeat. At that moment, I wanted to run to him and give him the longest hug. Was he alone? Should I sit with him? Would that be infringing on his personal space?

"Miss Zeek," a female voice called. "It's ZICK," I politely corrected as I was escorted to the infusion room.

Mitomycin - C

Mitomycin was pretty in the syringe – it was lavender. Deceiving, like a killer in a pretty dress.

Mitomycin is an anti-cancer chemotherapy drug classified as an "antitumor antibiotic." As a lab rat by profession, I was stunned to learn that this drug was developed from a fungus in the soil (Streptomyces)!

It's primarily used to treat adenocarcinoma of the stomach or pancreas. It is also used to treat many other cancers, including anal cancers.

If a drug is mainly used to treat certain cancers, but physicians believe the potential benefits outweigh the risk of using it to treat another cancer, it is utilized.

My nurse, Carolanne, was a woman about forty years old with a hairstyle older than her age and a quiet disposition. She pulled up a chair, sat before me, and gave me the purple killer over twenty minutes to ensure a slow and steady push. IV administration is the only way to get it because it doesn't come in a pill form. Mitomycin will cause vast tissue damage for weeks or months if it gets outside the vein. That is why the syringe was labeled "vesicant."

Nausea and vomiting are common side effects, and they can be severe. My physician gave me an anti-nausea drip before the chemo. It worked, and I was fine. So far, so good. Other side effects can be stomach/abdominal pain,

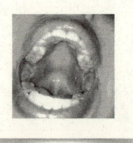

SORES IN MY THROAT

loss of appetite, dehydration, and hair loss. I read that pain or sores in the mouth and throat may occur, and they did. I developed horrendous sores in my mouth and throat.

It was raw appearing, and I could barely swallow saliva, let alone a meal. Dr. Michael prescribed a 2% lidocaine gel that was "swish and swallow." It numbed my throat enough that I managed to get some food down. It continued this way for the entirety of my treatments. Even the blandest foods felt like gasoline being washed over the rawness.

Follow-up testing for chemo was routine blood draws to monitor my blood counts and liver and kidney functions. I had lab appointments prior to each of my checkups with Dr. Michael.

Chemo works by damaging the RNA or DNA of cancerous cells. That way, the cell is confused about how to replicate itself. If the cells can't divide, tumor growth should stop or slow. Unfortunately, chemotherapy cannot distinguish between tumor cells and normal cells. The typical cell areas most affected by chemo are red and white blood cells, hair follicles, stomach, bowel, and mouth. That's why chemo induces low blood counts, mouth sores, hair loss, nausea, and diarrhea. That makes sense, right?

Like everything else, there are things we should and shouldn't do, and I learned as I went. Below is a list for Mitomycin (these apply to 5-fluorouracil as well). Many of these are to reduce the risk of bleeding. We could lose significant blood, internally or externally, should our platelet count drop.

Recommended "dos" and "don'ts" during mitomycin [2]

DO	DON'T
Drink 2-3 quarts fluids/day	Conceive a child
Wash hands often	Breastfeed
Avoid crowds/infection risk	Drink alcohol
Use an electric razor	Get unapproved immunizations
Use a soft toothbrush	Play contact sports
Avoid sun exposure	Wait until you're hungry to eat – Eat on a schedule
Get plenty of rest	
Maintain good nutrition Eat more protein	Take probiotics

Contact your healthcare team immediately if you experience a fever of 100.5° F (38° C) or higher or begin to have chills. You may be getting an infection, so let them know. Please don't put it off.

---

2.   Santhakumar, Sasha. "11 Things Not To Do During Chemotherapy." *Medical News Today.* www.medicalnewstoday.com/articles/things-not-to-do-while-on-chemotherapy-what-to-avoid#summary, September 14, 2021, Accessed 18 Feb 2024.

5-Fluorouracil (5-FU)

5-FU was in a take-home fanny pack that automatically dispensed in microdoses through my PICC line. 5-Fluorouracil is

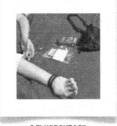

5-FLUOROURACIL

classified as an "antimetabolite." Antimetabolites are a lot like normal substances in a cell, but when this chemo enters the cellular metabolism, the normal cells can no longer divide. What happens is that the 5-fluorouracil messes with DNA and RNA synthesis by imitating what they need for cell reproduction.

Fluorouracil is also used to treat many cancers: gastrointestinal cancers, breast, head, neck cancer, and many others. But, unlike Mitomycin, this chemo can be found in creams for skin cancers.

My black bag containing the 5-FU was my partner around the clock for four days. To the dinner table? Of course, it's a fabulous idea to have a bold, lettered **CAUTION** label next to my food. Carry it to bed? Absolutely, but not the bed partner I've always dreamed of. {eye roll} The shower?! Like a monkey juggling bananas, I also took it to the shower.

I named it "Poison Patty" because she reminded me of her presence every few seconds with her haunting and eurythmic sound. << click. click. click. >>

I fell apart emotionally, and I was a helpless onlooker. My hair began to fall out. At first, there were a few noticeable hairs on the top I was wearing. Next, I began to notice more in the hairbrush. Tears rained pretty hard when I saw bigger clumps in the shower.

But the overwhelming breaking point was when I got up from the exam table at the hospital, and there were chunks (nearly handfuls) on the pillow.

But, "It's just hair."

It's MY HAIR. It is part of MY FEMINITY! ("But it will grow back," I tried to console myself) MAYBE. MAYBE NOT.

You don't understand! That - it - that hair… is a part of me! And I cannot control what is happening. I CAN'T EVEN CONTROL MY EMOTIONS RIGHT NOW.

Where is that Zoloft that I didn't need?

Bursting into tears, I wanted to empty the bottle.

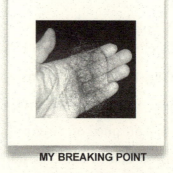

MY BREAKING POINT

Chemo Side Effects

Both chemo drugs can potentially cause so many side effects, and I encountered many. I will list the ones I experienced first and share how I came to manage each.

What I experienced

- **Nausea**

Zofran

In the beginning, this medication effectively controlled my nausea.

Ativan

When the Zofran wasn't adequate, I called my oncology team. My doctor told me to take an Ativan. Not feeling well, and out of exasperation, I clarified to the good doctor that "I am not anxious! I am desperately nauseated!" And, very gently, he explained to me that Ativan helps with nausea, too. Humbly, I shut up. Sometimes I need to be shut up.

- **Diarrhea**

Imodium, liquid

I drank it straight from the bottle, seemingly all day, every day. If there were an industrial-sized bottle, I would've bought that, along with a beer bong and a five-foot hose.

The chemo killed the "good" gut bacteria, and I acquired an incessant C. Difficile infection.

That is the NASTIEST, WATERIEST, ICKIEST, MOST FOUL-SMELLING DIARRHEA you ever want to meet— and the remedy was an anti-parasitic medication.

If you ever get C. diff, be sure to keep your towels separate from others in the household and wash your hands a lot! That crap is crazy contagious! Mint oil was the only thing I found to mask the smell even a little. I put enough of it on a cotton ball to soak it and dropped it into a small disposable paper cup, placing it up high so nobody could touch it and catch my cooties.

- **Mouth sores and decreased appetite**

<u>Two percent lidocaine gel</u>

Swish and swallow - this numbs the mouth and throat enough for food to follow. (I thought my lack of appetite was because of the sores.)

- **Metal taste**

The taste of metal in the mouth

(After hearing and reading about the dreaded metal taste, I mistakenly thought that it would occur when I ate certain foods or when using metal utensils, but no, it was ALL THE TIME — as if I continually gnawed on a wad of aluminum foil!) Chemo chemicals are present in the saliva when it attacks cancer and other cells. Some patients have a complete change in taste reception. I was fortunate; I only had a metal mouth.

<u>Hard ginger candy</u>

It helped to some degree, but I found something better (for me)

<u>Lemon heads candy</u>

This helped mask the metal taste a lot! I probably ate a million of them. Maybe two million.

- **Thinning Hair and Hair Loss**

<u>Cut it</u>

I had sat up from the radiation table. Although the techs hadn't yet turned the lights on, and only a trickle of light peeked through the control room, I could see so much hair on the pillowcase. Through eyes welling up, I looked to the girls and asked where the nearest hair salon was.

They knew why I was asking. And they, agreeing, had an immediate suggestion, complete with directions. As I sat in Sabrina's chair, she made no presumptions. Her hair was beautiful, and she had a lovely disposition. I wanted to hate her. But I didn't. Her smile was beautiful and genuine. "What are we doing today?" she cheerfully asked. I bet she always had this sunny disposition. "Shave it," was all I could say aloud. I hung my head, hoping *Sunny Sabrina* didn't see my tears. "Ahhhh," she said with understanding. "I have an idea. Why don't you let me cut it short, and if it doesn't look thicker and fuller, or if you don't like it, I will shave it for you. But let's try this first, okay?"

"Whatever," I replied. By the time she was finished, my tired eyes had dried, and I liked it; I thanked her, she didn't charge me a penny, and I gave Sunny Sabrina a long (happy) tearful hug.

Wigs

The Cancer Center where I was treated had wigs donated to them for other survivors to wear. It was an excellent service, and there was a private room to try them on. There were hats, scarves, and beanies too.

I learned losing my hair was profoundly painful. I didn't want it to be. I permitted myself to feel those emotions though. And wasn't in vain. It's acceptance of who I was in the moment. So, I tried on some wigs, and I went home with the one I got married in two months later.

- **<u>Low blood counts</u>**

<u>Red blood cells (RBCs)</u>

Purpose - Carries oxygen from the lungs to other parts of the body.

Deficiency - Decreased RBCs cause your body to work harder to get oxygen. You'll feel tired and short of breath.

My red cells and hemoglobin dropped but weren't at a critically low level. Should the numbers drop to a critical level, a transfusion of packed red blood cells could be required. The units would be tested to ensure it is free of HIV, Hepatitis B / C, West Nile Virus, etc. Transfusions are very safe.

<u>White blood cells (WBCs)</u>

Purpose - There are five different types of WBCs and a routine blood count, conducted by the lab, checks the numbers in all five classes. White blood cells help your body fight bacterial infections and other "intruders," such as viruses and parasites.

Deficiency - My count steadily dropped from $7.8 \rightarrow 4.2 \rightarrow 0.9$, which is critically low value.

I took injections of a white blood cell growth stimulator. The injections prompted my bone marrow to make WBCs again. I gave the injections to myself. The solution burned as it was injected, so I pushed the medication slowly. Don't judge. I was going through enough. This one small thing I could control.

After my injections, my white count began increasing. Then it skyrocketed from 1.3 → 1.4 → 27.2 which is critically high. So, I saw both ends of the scale. Finally, it stabilized within the normal range of 3.5-11.0

Platelets

Purpose - Platelets are the cells that make a clot and stop your body from bleeding uncontrollably. If you've cut yourself while shaving, platelets were on the scene to begin the clotting process.

Deficiency - If you have a deficiency of platelets, you may notice that you bruise very easily, cuts or nosebleeds won't stop bleeding, menstrual cycles are extraordinarily heavy, you could see reddish-purple pinpoint dots (petechiae) on your arms or legs, or blood in stool, etc.

You may require a platelet transfusion. My platelets dropped, but fortunately, not to a critical level. Platelets can also be transfused.

- **Rash**

This was the first side effect I experienced. It was more like little pimples around my forehead, and it occurred within two days of my first round of chemo. This wasn't uncomfortable for me; it was slightly itchy and an infringement on my vanity, but that's it.

- **Canker sores**

I had little sores inside my lips, but I wouldn't say they were canker sores. They didn't grow like a cold sore would. I had the "sore" part down, though. My lips felt very full and irritated. The back of my throat had variable red and white patches that manifested as miserable raw sores. Being dehydrated (because they were so sore that I didn't drink enough) didn't help my cause.

- **Infection**

The only infection I had was Clostridium difficile (C.Diff), and that information was included under the diarrhea heading.

- **Heartburn or Stomach ulcer**

I was given Prilosec during a hospital stay. At that point, I had upper GI pain, and I was diagnosed with GERD. I still take Prilosec ten years later and have now been diagnosed with Barret's esophagus (a pre-malignant condition). So far, studies do not link chemotherapy to the onset of Barret's.

- **Weakness/Low energy**

Rest was the only thing recommended. And I gave it reasonable effort. Unfortunately, my pre-cancer energy and stamina never returned. Other survivors have told me that they only came back to 70-80 percent of what they were pre-cancer, regardless of what they tried. Others say good diet and exercise ultimately made them better than ever.

Recently, I tried mushroom coffee; it seems to be helping me energy-wise. If you're struggling with fatigue and lack of energy, check with your physician and consider trying it.

- **Other**

A Stroke?

I did have a couple of disturbing incidents that were related to my chemotherapy. I had episodes of slurred speech caused by a "frozen" tongue. I described those episodes as "stroke-like" symptoms. My tongue felt rigid, and I couldn't get any words out. My mind knew what I wanted to say, but I couldn't talk. I felt stupid when the words wouldn't come. It was highly frustrating and a little scary. My wonderful oncologist took my concerns seriously and sent me to an oncology neurologist as a precaution. Thankfully, I only had a few of these episodes.

Oddly, the neurologist didn't seem to be alarmed. I suppose he had seen enough of these incidents to recognize the related symptoms. After having an MRI, he assured me that I hadn't had a stroke. (These episodes were determined to be "Chemotherapy Adverse Reactions - Spell of Transient Neurologic Symptoms.")

[Note: I haven't had any more of these occurrences since finishing chemo.]

I was checked regularly by my health care team while I was taking chemotherapy to monitor side effects and check my response to therapy. Periodic blood work was obtained to monitor my complete blood count (CBC) and tests to monitor the function of my other organs (such as kidneys and liver) were carried out. I had blood work done with every appointment.

Germ awareness

Being extra cautious with potential infection sources was crucial. We are susceptible to infections during treatments, which could be extremely dangerous. One often-ignored source of bacteria for women is their makeup applicators.

Disposable applicator kits are available to ensure as much cleanliness as possible.

DISPOSABLE SPONGES, LIP AND MAS-CARA WANDS, SHADOW APPLICATORS, ETC.

Chapter 9

RADIATION. BEEN THERE, FRIED THAT.

For me; radiation was the worst part of my treatment. Despite being provided with a significant amount of reading material and making an effort to go through it, I was overwhelmed. And, at that time, stress might not have allowed me to grasp the information fully. The consequence was staggering, a forceful punch in the gut that knocked the wind out of me. Instinctively, I clutched my gut in pain and fell into the fetal position on the floor. I had a lot of battle scars, and bitterness washed over me. I realized later that the information on the side effects did not sink in. Would I have continued if I'd known "then" what I know "now"?

Well, because cancer was new to me at that time, I still would've chosen to have both chemo and radiation as my treatment. The combination of the two is known as the Nigro Protocol, and it's the "gold standard" for anal cancer. Every weekday, Paul drove me an hour and a half to the cancer center to receive my daily dose of gamma rays. The first few weeks weren't bad at all.

Painless. I did notice the flesh becoming a bit pink, and my pubic hair was falling out. Near the end of my treatment, in week five, I had terrible burns from the radiation. My external flesh was raw and seeping. Internally, it was even worse as I had essentially been cooked from the inside out. I screamed with pain when urine passed through my tract. (And let me add, I know what pain is; I've had a thoracotomy with lung resection, so I learned what ten pain was). It was unbearable agony. Especially when going to the bathroom. I didn't want to drink anything because I didn't want to pee. But that made things worse because the urine was more concentrated, which caused even more pain. It was torturous and intolerable. I immediately contacted Dr. Michael, who instructed me to meet him at the emergency room.

My cancer hospital is a teaching hospital. Residents everywhere. Upon admission, a nurse needed to look at "*the area.*" I heard, "Oh my!" exclaimed, and then Nurse Cinthya left my room. Shortly after, a doctor, accompanied by a medical student, wanted to see it. And then another doctor had her turn, and so on. I finally had enough of displaying myself to all the staff. When another nurse came into my room, I sarcastically asked her if she thought she could find anyone else in the hallway that might need to see because I think everyone in three counties has already been in to visit *the area*?!" I was rude, and I was snarling with anger stemming from agony. She quickly apologized for what I'd been through. I felt ashamed and… I hurt. I HURT A LOT. And I was at the point where all I could do was cry. I needed help, and I was there for them to help me, not for me to show my raw stuff to a bunch of strangers to gawk at. I was hospitalized for eight days to get the pain under control. After several days, the pain was somewhat manageable with morphine. Lots and lots of morphine. During my stay, I found that if I used the morphine release pump as much as was permissible before going to pee, I could do it without too much screaming. It was truly horrible. It wasn't just the pain. It was the fatigue, the dread, the feeling of defeat. Upon my release from the hospital, I was utterly exhausted; my skin was raw and weeping, and pieces of flesh were hanging from my groin. I decided that I could not go through one more day of radiation. Reluctantly, I told my fiancé. For the first time since being diagnosed, I was quitting. Or so I thought.

When I arrived home that Thursday evening, there was a voicemail from the cancer center. My oncology radiologist gave me a short break, which allowed me to heal further. Instead of returning the next day, I was scheduled to go back on Monday. Thank you, Jesus! I was allowed a three-day reprieve to heal, and consequently, I was able to finish my final treatments. I DID IT. IT WAS OVER!

Looking forward to ringing the end-of-treatment bell, I walked straddle-legged into the waiting room. This was a moment to look forward to; my completion and a massive encouragement to every other patient in the room. When I pushed the door open, only a few lights were on, and no one was in the waiting room. I was the last patient. There went my joy. There was no one to share it with. No one for me to encourage. No one to share my excitement with. No one to congratulate me. Paul allowed me to sulk momentarily as he rounded up some staff to be photographed with me as I rang that bell. I rang it loud and proud.

Now, let's address some FAQs:

1. What is radiation therapy, in a general sense?

Your treatment team will use high doses of radiation to kill, or at least slow down, the cancer to stop it from spreading. It's like an X-ray, only stronger. And it's targeted to a more specific area than an X-ray of your back. Laser beams are used in conjunction with tiny tattooed dots (yes, seriously) to target the exact location of the cancer every time accurately.

About 60 percent of all cancer patients need radiation treatments. You'll have a protective shielding mask if you have head or neck radiation.

2. Does this treatment affect healthy cells?

Yes. Although targeted to a specific area, it does affect/damage nearby healthy cells. When deciding on your treatment regimen, the oncology radiologist determines the lowest dose that can be used to kill cancer cells.

3. Is radiation always coupled with chemo?

No. Depending on the type of cancer, it can be used alone, before, during, and following surgery.

4. How long does it take for the effects of radiation to work?

It is not immediate, like chemo. It takes days to weeks before the cancer cells begin to die after radiotherapy. And once it starts, it continues for weeks, or even months, after you've finished.

5. Are there different kinds of radiation?

Yes. There's "external" radiation, like an X-ray, and "internal" radiation. Internal radiation therapy requires either a liquid (which you drink) or some target device (a capsule or a seed) to be implanted in your body at the cancer site. It's usually put into place through a catheter or some other applicator.

Cancer. A Journey Of A Thousand Miles.

6. Do I have to have a specific diet during treatment?

Although not "required," maintaining a healthy weight is essential. Calories! Protein! It takes a lot of energy to HEAL. Talk with your oncology radiologist or a dietician for more specific guidelines.

7. Will I be able to continue working while going through treatment?

There's not a definitive "yes" or "no" here. Many factors determine the answer. The significant factors are the type of treatment, whether coupled with chemotherapy, and how your body handles it.

8. If I have external radiotherapy, am I going to be radioactive?

No. But there are precautions for internal radiation once it's in place. Your oncology team will keep you informed of those.

9. What side-effects might I experience?

Fatigue and some degree of skin changes (dry, itchy, a "sunburn," or even blistering skin) are usually inevitable. The set radiation dose and the number of treatments required are factors that can determine how quickly side effects appear.

Depending on where your cancer is, the following may be an issue (and I was very surprised to learn some of them): hair loss at the radiation site, nausea and vomiting, diarrhea, swelling, swallowing problems, changes in sexual function or fertility, pain, taste changes, and urinary/bladder/bowel problems.

The good news is that most of these will disappear within a couple of months after the completion of radiation treatments. Radiology was the department where I felt like part of a cattle herd. They were so organized and had everything timed to a T. And to a fault. After checking in and a quick visit with the radiation oncologist, I returned to the main waiting area. Within minutes, I'd be called back to the hallway waiting area. It was an on-deck chair where I waited for the patient before me to be radiated. After that patient walked past me, I was called back to the treatment room, where the techs were sterilizing the exam/testing table. This department was quick, precise, and regimented. When they motioned to me seconds later, one tech helped me onto the table while another retrieved my leg mold. "Okay, Laura, bend those knees and get settled in." As I did that, another was pulling a sheet over me from my knees to my chest. "Do you need any help getting your pants down?" My pants had to be pulled below where I'd be radiated. "No, thank you. I've got it".

Quickly, they lined my tattooed dots up with the laser beams projected from the walls. After re-checking beam alignment to ensure perfection, they raised the table, confirmed my settings on the machine's computer were correct, and left the room. As the treatment began, the arms of this beastly machine began to slowly rotate around my midsection, going from above me to my left side, behind me to the right side, and returning to the start position. I counted each click of the machine until I inevitably knew how many clicks were in each quarter section. Sometimes, the rhythmic clicking put me to sleep. Yeah, I was that tired. There was no pain, burning, or sensation of any kind. The entire radiating process took about three to five minutes. As I left the treatment room, the next patient was called in from the on-deck chair.

I wondered, was I the only one who felt like herded cattle?

Chapter 10

I DO.
I REALLY DO.

At 10:30 on the morning of April 6, 2013, I disconnected the chemo from the PICC line hanging from the inside of my right bicep. Gathering my thoughts, wig, makeup bag, and some gorgeous jewelry, I headed to the church. The sun shone brightly, and it felt glorious on my face. A perfect day for a wedding!

My simple ivory dress was already in the little parlor, and my anticipation began to build. It wouldn't be a big event, but it would be as elegant as I could afford. And I put everything together in less than two months while going through treatments! To me, that was incredible.

I designed distinctive red, black, and ivory invitations, uti-  lizing an online printing service for their production. Our church pianist graciously agreed to provide the music and included my request for "Love Story" to be played. A dear friend of Paul's captured the photographs of our special day, and we weren't disappointed. The images were perfect. As for the programs and guestbooks, I created

115

them, including a canvas with an (obviously amateur) painted tree motif where guests would leave their fingerprints as leaves and sign their names below. My sisters prepared wedding cupcakes to complement the theme, and the extraordinary ladies from our church generously catered an outstanding meal for the reception, held in the church's banquet hall.

The reception was also understated. My son put together a video of our "story" thus far and played it at the reception. He did a great job. It had very apropos music (God Blessed the Broken Road). At the end, there was a comical "Produced by" credit with his name, which made me smile.

I'd slipped on my ivory stockings but wasn't inclined to get out of my comfy clothes. But the clock's hands continued to march forward, so I began applying my makeup. I even wore false eyelashes! I thought they were lovely. Not gaudy or obnoxiously bougie, but just enough to bring out the joy in my weary eyes.

Carefully placing the wig onto my head, I made some ad-justments, and Donna, naturally by my side as my maid of honor,

Warrior, arise! Arise NOW!

walked into the room and gave an approving smile. She did the honors of putting the little pearl tiara onto my head. Upon donning my sleeveless dress and ivory lace cape, I felt prettier than I had since that cancer beast came after me.

People invariably say that cancer pa-tients are warriors. I never felt like that. But right then, I needed to become a warrior. I knew I would be getting tired and my strength sapped. I did not want my wedding day to feel like a fight. I wanted to have joyous memories.

Deep in my soul, my mind called out, "Warrior, arise! ARISE NOW!!" I needed her for the day ahead.

Our photographer, Lynn, walked in. That girl is just naturally happy. Disgustingly happy. All. The. Time. So, at that moment, I smiled and pulled up some energy from my toes, and I was the happiest girl in the whole world.

I had previously told Lynn about some specific humorous pictures I wanted to be taken, and we did those first. I stretched out on the sofa with a couple of prescription pill bottles in hand, had a fan blowing onto my face, and Donna was wiping my brow. The idea was to portray pre-wedding anxiety as a joke. For my handsome groom, his best man, Jerry, was captured, taking his pulse. They were cute images. They were fun. They were, and still are beautiful memories.

Guests began arriving around 12:30 p.m. for the 1:00 ceremony. But there was a SLIGHT PROBLEM. My sons, who were to walk me down the aisle to take my vows, had not yet arrived. Ummm, they knew what time to be there. Paul gave them directions. "You just go like you're going through Elkdale and follow the signs north to our town. Go through the light (there's only one stoplight), make the next left, and then the second left. The church is two blocks away. On the left." It wasn't that difficult. Plus, they had a GPS. So, being concerned that something happened, I called. "Where are you guys?" I asked, trying to be nonchalant. My younger son, not so calmly, responded, "Well, mom, we don't really know. I guess we're lost because we just saw a sign that said 'prison - 10 miles'."

"Mom?"

Swallowing hard I said, "Yeh, I'm here. Turn around. You went waaaay too far; you're about an hour away."

"I don't know how we got lost. Paul said, 'Go through Elkdale and follow the signs.' We didn't see any signs."

"Not CLEAR THROUGH Elkdale." <<jeesh>> "TO Elkdale. It doesn't matter. Just turn around and get here." I laughed. (Paul knew what he meant; he didn't clarify it for someone unfamiliar with that area.)

"Sorry, Mom." <<click>>

I will admit I wasn't very relaxed after hanging up. I'd been working relentlessly on gratitude and letting go of circumstances I had no control over. Everything was going to be okay. Even if no guests showed up, even if all the guests left, I would still get married, and a life of togetherness would begin. Our pastor explained to the guests why the ceremony hadn't yet started. By this time, my eighty-seven-year-old future father-in-law was nervously tapping the back of the pew with his foot and pointing a stern index finger at his watch. His military training had taught him to always be on time. "It's after 1:00", he reminded Paul. "What is going on? You were supposed to be married twenty minutes ago." His impatience had him ready to leave. "Dad! Laura's boys are on their way. You have nothing else to do today, and you've seen every *Gunsmoke* episode, so sit back down and relax."

About fifty minutes later, both boys walked their somewhat nervous, wig-wearing, cancer-fighting mom down the aisle  to meet her awaiting husband. No one said anything to us about the late start, but I imagine there was more than one impatient guest. It was a beautiful ceremony. We chose to include a memory candle to honor my father and Paul's mother, both of whom had passed away many years ago. A unity sand ceremony was also conducted. Simultaneously, we each poured different colors of sand into a glass vase. Keeping with our color scheme, I poured white, and Paul poured red. It represented our two separate lives coming together as one. Our sand was beautiful when poured up to the top of the clear, cylindrical, heart-shaped vase. We said our "Do you takes?" and "I dos," and then he kissed me just like he did for our first kiss. He, oh so gently, cupped my face into his hands and brought me near to him. "I DO! I REALLY DO!" my tears screamed.

At our reception, the cupcakes were a huge hit. People still talk about them to this day! My sister found a wedding cake recipe for cupcakes, and they were *incredible*. Each perfect little cup-

cupcake was beautifully adorned with pearl-like edibles and light-reflecting iridescent flakes. The cupcakes were tiered into a cake shape. The top tier was a small layer cake we saved for our first anniversary. It was well-wrapped for us and well-eaten the following year.

The video played repeatedly for guests to watch at their leisure. Our perpetually happy photographer continued snapping away, capturing some priceless candid moments. My sister, Ann, gave a congratulatory toast that she nearly didn't get out because of happy tears. We are an expressive and emotional bunch! Either that, or we are just super hormonal at this time in our lives. It could very well be the latter.

My sons left relatively early (show up late and leave early, as the saying goes), but I had "pre-approved" this because the boys had tickets to see Eric Clapton in Pittsburgh that evening. So, after nearly forcing a few not-so-photographic smiles for mother/son photos, they took off for a fun-filled night with an extraordinary musician and entertainer.

I was wearing down, and my inner warrior had betrayed me. It wasn't until I clearly saw in the wedding pictures that my strength had faded. But that's okay. I had just completed chemo and still had several radiation treatments to go. And I now had an incredible man, a husband, to help me through that — and the rest of my life. That deserves an "amen" or a "woohoo" or "yippee ky yay" or something. (Thanks)

120

Chapter 11

IT'S NEVER OVER

Following all the chemotherapy and radiation treatments, it was necessary to undergo thorough and consistent monitoring. This was a regimen of either a PET/CT scan or a colonoscopy. These two types of testing were alternated every six months over the next five years. This was to ensure no malignant activity was going on within me. It sounds simple enough, right? It wasn't. My body had been destroyed. Destructed at the cellular level by chemotherapeutic drugs. Cooked from the inside out by radiation. But, my medical team (and myself) needed to know that all was well within me and that it would stay that way.

I had finished radiation treatments in April, so in July, I had my scheduled PET/CT scan to look for any hot spots. This was when I had my first encounter with scanxiety. Scanxiety is a term used to convey the anxiety associated with follow-up scans. In two days, Dr. Michael called me at home. I sat down weak-kneed, and I'm sure he heard the nervousness in my voice. "Congratulations!" he enthusiastically exclaimed. "There is no evidence of any cancer in your scan." Although I nearly collapsed, I thanked him graciously for calling me with this fantastic news. Shortly after that, I headed to work. It was a warm, sunny day, so Paul encouraged me to drive the sports car. "I already have the top down for you." I just had to oblige, right? And with an especially tender hug, I kissed Paul goodbye and carefully negotiated the steps as I left for work. Neighbors were mowing their lawns, and children were being called in for lunch by their mothers. The smell of cut grass tickled my nose, but it wasn't a worry. No time for allergy concerns – I was cancer-free. Cancer was a beast, but so was I!

Never had I given such sincere thanks to God. I drove hard and fast. I was deliriously happy. And I didn't care who heard me as I drove down the road screaming, "The cancer is gone! DO YOU HEAR ME, WORLD? THE CANCER IS GONE!! Thank you, God! THANK YOU! GOD!"

I soaked up the sunshine, which kept me happy all day. Bursting at the seams, I shared the news with coworkers, and other staff members and received congratulations and warm hugs. One sincere and congratulatory well wish came from Dr. Ted, one of the Department heads. His sincerity meant the world to me. It was an extraordinary day.

My next follow-up test was in October. Since they alternated quarterly, I was scheduled for a colonoscopy at that time. I did the prep; however, the surgeon found that I wasn't completely emptied. The scoping process was aborted upon reaching the "uncleared" portion of my colon. I was distraught upon hearing this news because everything was running clear, as it should be. It was quite a while before I learned how and why that occurred, and I'll explain that in the next section.

Pray that I don't wake up

I had some discouraging and overwhelming times because with EVERY colonoscopy came tubular adenomas. Those are the "bad" polyps that, if left in the colon, could potentially become malignancies. I seem to be a superhero at making them, overachiever that I am. I can't just make one and be done; I've got to show off and make three or more.

My mood became quite depressive, knowing that these polyps would most likely kill me at some point. That, coupled with the ongoing post-therapy issues, often proved to be too much for me emotionally. It'd been about five years of having colonoscopies every six months. Because of the inability to get thoroughly cleaned out, I was required to do a two-day prep with every scope. These were not two partial prep days; they were two complete bowel preps in two consecutive days. For example, if my colonoscopy is scheduled on a Monday, I would begin the Dulcolax and Miralax prep on Saturday. I have no sphincter squeeze power, so in the bathroom I sit until I run out of liquid waste. Then, on Sunday morning, I do the same thing, from start to finish. I know that five years out of 57 (at the time) is minimal (not even 10 percent of my life), but in those five years, it had been all I'd known. What was wrong with me? Or, more appropriately, what had the radiotherapy done to my anatomy? I knew

123

that most other survivors weren't being tormented like this. Or, if they were, they weren't making it publically known.

After much consideration and despair, I talked with my oncologist during my next appointment. I am blessed because he LISTENS to my concerns. He takes them seriously and does not dismiss them as soon as the words leave my tongue.

Dr. Michael proposed that I see a GI Surgical specialist. I was told that this physician was outstanding and that he could likely help me. Terrific news!

When I had my appointment with Dr. Herschel, I left his office in tears of joy and hope. This man explained to me what had happened physiologically to my body! I finally understood it!

A "normal" rectum has a muscular tone. Mine has virtually no tone because of the radiation damage. A "normal" anal canal is about an inch to 1.25" in diameter when distended. Mine, let's say that my miniature schnauzer pooped bigger turds than I did. That's the truth! It's called **STENOSIS** (a canal narrowing because of scar tissue and decreased blood flow).

Now, back to the physiologic problem — in the body, undigested (solid) waste is processed through the stomach, the small intestine (where it mixes with bile from the liver and enzymes from the pancreas), and then what is unable to be digested moves on to the large intestine. There, the colon absorbs water from stool, making it a more solid stool. That stool then moves to the sigmoid colon, where it is stored until one needs to "go," and it passes through the rectum and out the anus. That's in a non-radiated body.

Everything moves along great for me until things get to the sigmoid colon. Things stop there, and a "plug" forms. So, I didn't have a bowel movement for days. Too much information?

Oh, it gets much worse. Stop reading now if you don't want to know.

The two-day preps overcome this. Because of the plug formation, when prepping, everything runs clear like the surgeon wants, but I'm not "clean" because all the clear liquid is snaking AROUND THE PLUG. Then, during the procedure, the colonoscopy has to be aborted because they cannot see past the sigmoid colon.

Because I have urgency on a *regular day* and little control on a *regular day*, I cannot leave the bathroom for the larger part of two consecutive days when prepping. I do manage to stand on occasion. But that is it. After drinking my laxative, I do not want to drink another ounce because I do not want to be in the bathroom one second longer than necessary. My legs always feel badly bruised. My booty becomes raw and it bleeds. Once, I was admitted to the hospital with a critically low potassium because I was so dehydrated. I take a heater and blankets into the bathroom because losing fluids causes me to get extremely cold. I take pillows to lay on my clothes hamper to have a collapsing nap when possible. My phone and laptop go with me. Anything to help the next forty-eight hours to be a little more manageable goes to the bathroom with me.

After visiting with Dr. Herschel, I had **hope** because I now understood what was happening inside me. After explaining it all, he asked me to take Metamucil daily and a stool softener twice daily. I looked at the man like he had three heads! He must've seen that look before because he said, "I know. You have incontinence problems, and I want you to take a stool softener." Then he added that after doing that for two weeks, he wanted me to drink a bottle of magnesium sulfate (a laxative) on my day off and to continue this weekly pattern until my next colonoscopy — which was scheduled with him in six weeks. I'll admit, I wasn't thrilled, but if it was going to FIX ME, I would do about anything.

Surprisingly, the recommended Metamucil and stool softener routine went well. Two weeks later, on a Sunday afternoon, I drank the laxative. I knew I'd probably be stuck in the bathroom for an hour or so, and I got my survival kit together and closed the door. Nine hours later, I was still in there! It was like a complete bowel prep, and I decided that I'd had enough. I was not doing this again. EVER. **IF I DIE, I DIE**. I always got so sick, so depleted, so overwhelmingly and irrationally depressed.

Around midnight, I was finally able to shuffle to bed. My husband and I always pray together at night, and like every night, he asked if there were any special prayer needs I knew of.

Sobbing uncontrollably, I said, "Just pray that I don't wake up in the morning." I had surrendered. I couldn't do it again. I just wanted to go to sleep and never wake up.

But I did wake up. I supposed I still have a purpose.

Chapter 12

ha

SCANXIETY. . . AND OTHER NOT-SO-MEDICAL TERMS

O n a lighter note, I will soon be bilingual. It's true. I've learned a whole new vocabulary. And, to show you that my heart is in the right place, I will share what I've learned with you so you can also be bilingual. Here we go alphabetically (because I'm "anal").

Anal Cancer Terms and Their Meanings

Anal buds – anal cancer buddies.

Baconated – skin fried crispy like bacon (radiation damage).

Bag lady – a woman with an ileostomy or colostomy bag.

BMWs – bowel movement worries.

Cancerversary – can be the anniversary date of your diagnosis or the anniversary date of being NED (defined later).

[Personal note: I originally designated my cancerversary date to be the latter because I wanted it to be celebratory. But I have changed my mind. Why? Because my diagnosis date will always be my diagnosis date. And I'm not so naïve as to think it will never come back. So, if that would be the case, I hope to have more than one CANCER-FREE date. But the day I learned I had cancer will never change. I CHOSE a cancerversary date of January 8, 2013.]

Chemobrain — having trouble focusing, interpreting, and articulating thoughts. Memory/thinking problems after chemo. It may be short-term or long-term.

Chemocrop — the short hairstyle women often have when undergoing or recently completed chemotherapy.

Chemorrhoids — Anal/rectal irritation caused by chemo.

Chemoflage — the wearing of wigs, drawing on of eyebrows, or anything to camouflage the effects of what chemo treatments have done.

District of brown — the anal canal

Flaming "A" — description of your bottom (during radiotherapy) when having a bowel movement. Burns like fire!

Flatudance — the little dance you do as you desperately squeeze your butt cheeks together, attempting to hold in a fart while quickly trying to leave the immediate area.

Home invasion — colonoscopy.

Lymphie — someone with lymphedema.

Mushroom Fart — a big, stinky fart that explodes out your pants and graciously leaves a lingering "fart radiation" for those around you.

NED — NED is not Ned, a guy. It's an acronym for "no evidence of disease."

Nerve gas — severely foul gas — deadly to those around you.

Nubbin — chest port.

Pooperazzi — the colonoscopy team's pictures of your colon.

OGD — Obsessive Googling Disorder.

Poop Chute — the anal/rectal canal.

Presults — preliminary results you try to coax from the technician(s) performing your scans or other tests.

ProGAStination — putting off passing gas for as long as possible.

Scanxiety — the anxiety associated with follow-up CT or PET scans.

Scope dope — the "twilight" medication they give you before being scoped.

Shotgun effect — the damage that occurs in other areas of your body as a result of treating another part.

Chapter 13

COLLATERAL DAMAGE

I wish I could say that I am completely and blissfully enjoying my "cure". I am not. The treatment for anal cancer is known for harshly draconian and long-term side effects.

I thought IT was over. The fear. The stress. The tests. The side effects. No. None of those are over. There's too much collateral damage. And I'm not just speaking of the chances of cancer returning. That shadow of fear will probably follow me for the rest of my life. But there has to be sunshine present to have a shadow. I will do my best to focus on that. The sun. The warm and magnificent sun. I will press on.

Daily, I fight the side effects of radiation, and they can be long-term, if not life-long. I will address my complications of radiation therapy later in this chapter ... I still, from time to time, have trouble dealing with it all. With that being said, I can almost hear someone saying, "My gosh, suck it up! You should be grateful to be alive instead of worrying about some SIDE EFFECT."

Believe me, I am thankful and have a tremendous amount of guilt with my moments of self-pity. God has been so good to me, and I am overwhelmed by His goodness and mercy. But I am human. I have my bitter or angry moments. And they're not pretty.

I was not prepared for the post-treatment sequelae that I would endure. Late side effects may present six months to 20+ years following treatment. That was difficult for me to wrap my head around. 20 years. Factors that have a bearing on long-term side effects include:

- Area being treated

- Whether or not chemo was administered

- The type of chemo drug

- If radiation was given and at what dose

- Your body's immune system

Latent side effects of chemo

Please note: that not all chemo will cause the following latent side effects

- Dental problems

- Early menopause

- Hearing loss

134

- Increased risk of other cancers later

- Inability to conceive a child

- Cardiac issues

- Some degree of loss of taste

- Reduced lung capacity

- Nerve impairment

- Memory and cognitive difficulties

- Gastrointestinal issues

- Osteoporosis

Latent side effects of Radiation

It's essential to recognize that the location undergoing treatment, length of treatment, and the irradiation dose can affect the presence or absence of these side effects.

- Dental decay

- Hypothyroidism

- Menopause (early)

- Cardiac problems

- Increased risk for other cancers at a later time

- Infertility

- Gastrointestinal problems

- Lung disease

- Memory and cognitive issues

- Lymphedema

- Increased risk for stroke

- Osteoporosis

As you can see, several concerns are in both lists.

At the risk of becoming a social pariah, I will delve into my latent side effects and share what has helped me manage them and live a more normal life.

Pulling up my big girl panties

Nobody told me. Nobody told me that the pelvic radiation would damage my sphincter. Nobody told me that pelvic radiation would damage my sphincter badly.

Of course, it was in the literature, but nobody told me I would have this long-lasting AND DEFINITIVE side effect. The information sheet touched upon it. "Possible side effects," it stated. You could experience "bowel and bladder problems."

Maybe it should have been written: You will have varying degrees of bowel and bladder incontinence. **You will have.**

I hate you, cancer!

I haven't had too much of a problem with bladder control. I have had some leakage when I am very active. This is called stress incontinence. And I couldn't feel the leakage, so I wore a little pad to catch any dribble. Not that big of a deal.

The bowel issue was completely different, and I was not emotionally prepared for the degree of humiliation that I experienced. My new companion was named Humiliation.

hu·mil·i·a·tion, noun

Synonyms: embarrassment, mortification, shame, indignity, and disgrace

Check√, Check √, Check√, Check √, and Check √

My first experience with bowel incontinence was in a public place. It was absolutely horrible. Picture this — Paul and I, as newlyweds, are out of town with a realtor, looking at a lovely house for possible purchase. Suddenly, oh no!! I felt the urgent cramping. Presuming I could use the homeowner's bathroom for this emergency, I gave Paul a look of terror. Quickly, he asked the realtor if I could use … NO. The water had been turned off at this house!!! Wearing a look of hysteria and anguish on my face, I forcefully grabbed my husband by the arm and said, "We have to go NOW!" But I had an accident before we made it to our vehicle. And because of the undeniable stench, I'm sure the realtor knew what had happened, although he did not know WHY it happened. My pants were full, warm, and wet. I truly wanted to die. Right there. Just kill me. My once vibrant eyes were lost behind a veil of shame and tears. My husband desperately tried to console me, but I was angry. Very angry. Was this how it would be from now on?! I would have to become reclusive to salvage my dignity. It just didn't seem fair (whatever "fair" was). I worked diligently over the years to transform from an awkward waif-like teenager to a commanding persona sporting Vonda Doc Martens, an off-shoulder, knee-high denim dress, and prostitute red nails. I was confident in who I had evolved into over the years. But then, at that moment, I was forced to search for the ultimate panacea to show my face in public. I conceded that I was nothing more than a bag of dry bones kept together by helplessness.

Picture this one now… seriously, put yourself in my shoes (I haven't crapped in them yet). I had just finished my PET/CT scan at the hospital, and my husband and I stopped in Starbucks to grab a salted caramel latte to drink while commuting to my workplace. The glorious scent of freshly ground coffee beans tickled my nose. Deep inhale. Mmmm. Before my coffee was ready, I felt it. It was that all-familiar horrifying sensation of urgency. I had not even

138

taken two steps — **NOT TWO STEPS** — and it happened. Instantly. Right there in the middle of a crowded Starbucks, brimming with anxious and overly tired physicians, high-strung med students, weary patients, and visitors just wanting to get in and get out. Mortified, I ran (as inconspicuously as possible) to the nearest restroom. I was a disgusting, stinking, humiliated mess. From my phone, I told my husband I needed new scrubs because what I had on was unwearable. The gift shop at the hospital sold scrubs, so he promptly purchased me a get-away outfit and sent it to me by way of an older woman randomly passing by the restroom.

"*Laura?*" she called out.

"*Back here,*" I weakly replied from the handicapped stall. She quickly tossed the bag underneath the door and asked if I was okay as she fled towards the sink. I lied, saying,

"Yes, *I'm fine ... thanks for bringing this to me.*"

I was one hundred percent certain that she knew what had happened. I wanted to die. Right there in the restroom. I didn't care about how they would find me. I didn't care if the news would say, "*Woman Dies In Bathroom Stall After Hypoxic Suffocation From The Fumes Of Her Own Toxic Waste. Details at Eleven on WIFF News*". Why must I endure this? What is the purpose? Just so I can be completely transparent when encouraging other survivors? I don't want to do this any longer. I don't want the shame. I don't want first-hand experience. I don't; I can't do this. I'm not strong enough. I must be too proud. I just don't know.

It took me about half an hour to get cleaned up enough to wear the new scrubs and leave that restroom. We hurried to the car and headed toward work. Then, guess what? Yes. I did it once A G A I N! Could the night get any worse? I notified work that I would be later than anticipated, and we turned around and headed toward a friend's house where I could shower and do a quick wash/dry of the clothing. BUT IT DIDN'T END. So, yes, actually, the night COULD GET WORSE. How much was I to withstand? How much? And why at this moment? Could I not make it through a work night without a crapfest?

I ended up with a call-off and a miserable night, crying tears of shame. When we finally got home at 10:15 p.m., I went to the shower fully dressed. Yes, fully dressed and with poop everywhere, I slowly undressed. The exhaust fan was failing me. My sphincter failed me. My healthy attitude failed me. I was walking a vessel of waste under a waterfall shower. After rinsing out the clothes and getting myself clean, I sat beneath the showerhead, crying until there were no more tears. I showered again. At 11:30 p.m., I collapsed in the comfort of my bed. Paul bleached my tub for me. Some might say, "You couldn't help it," or "Everyone will have an accident at some point in their life." That's all true, but as I broke it down from my perspective:

for approximately the past 2,829 days,
which means,

for the past seven and three-quarter years (at the time this writing),

which means,

for nearly **20 percent** of my adult life (adult being 20 years old) ...

For nearly 20 percent of my life, I have been grieved by this consequence nearly every day.

I got weary. I was exhausted to the point where it took work to breathe – every breath in, every breath out. All of me was depleted.

Was I whining? No!

Was I exaggerating? N O!

Did I want a perfect life? N O – N O – N O!!!

But I had to find a way to manage and maintain whatever dignity I had remaining. I opted to down bottles of liquid anti-diarrhea medicine weekly. Even so, I had another public episode a couple of months later. I resigned to the fact that, at least for the time being, I would have to purchase and wear pull-ups. I <u>had</u> to. I just **_had_** to. I had to rescue my self-esteem, and I didn't want to keep throwing away beautiful and expensive panties.

"Goodbye, my exquisite Natori. Hello, dreadful De-pends". Disposable underwear. Diapers. Whatever you want to call them. I called them humiliating. I'd shed a lot of tears lately.

Despite being well-thought-of and respected in the community, I felt like I was living a lie, all put together on the outside but falling apart on the inside.

When I first began considering incontinence products, I envisioned a bulky adult diaper with layers upon layers of cotton-like absorbent pads. It would likely be covered with a plastic covering secured by tape tabs so that one size would fit all. It would make a distinct swish/swish noise as I walked or caused any movement against the plastic covering. And everyone would know! It was daunting and traumatizing.

After several experiences of emotional trauma, I began researching. I had no clue about the number of people going through the **same thing**. That both shocked and saddened me. Yet, no one seems to be openly discussing the issue. **IT NEEDS TO BE TALKED ABOUT**. This chapter is being written because of the prompting and encouragement of a reader and fellow anal cancer warrior.

So, what's a girl (or guy) to do? First, please understand that you are not alone. I am learning that nearly everyone who has had pelvic radiation experiences some degree of incontinence. So, whether or not people are openly sharing that information, it is occurring.

Secondly, stores like Walmart, Target, Walgreens, etc., carry incontinence products because they are needed. If there were no demand for them, the retail market would not carry them.

The issues can improve over time. Mine have. My urologist prescribed Vesicare to help with the bladder urgency and leaks. It's working wonderfully.

I searched for the best disposables option that I could find. I was pleasantly surprised to learn that there are close-fitting pull-up options in different colors; some have floral or lace prints, and some have a cloth-like waistband (so if it showed, it would be difficult to detect as an incontinence product). There are also washable incontinence panties that can be worn, washed and worn again.

After the initial shock and finding a brand I liked, the peace of mind was worth it. And I would imagine that this is better than having a colostomy bag. So …. I took a deep breath, pulled up my disposable big girl panties, and mustered up enough dignity to go on with life. Traveling now, even short distances, encompasses a sling backpack with an extra outfit, wet wipes, ziplock bags, a change of underwear, and a pull-up (for whatever the circumstance may call for).

What I discovered – first

Some chemotherapy drugs can cause bile acid malabsorption. Bile is made in the liver and is sent to the small intestine to help metabolize lipids (fats). If the body doesn't absorb and excrete the bile acid as it should, a surplus of water and watery stool will result.

My Primary Care Physician prescribed cholestyramine, an anti-lipid medication that also helps the absorption of bile acid. It comes in individual packets or a can. I mix one packet (or one scoop full) with my drink of choice, water. It can be combined with fruit juice, apple sauce, water, soda, or anything.

Oh HALLELUJAH! Hallelujah! And take the gun from my hands!

I am not even kidding. There were moments of weakness and exhaustion when I didn't want to fight anymore. I was tired of the anxiety of whether I would be able to make it from point "A" to point "B" without crapping right down my leg. I fought a silent and relentless monster called incontinence, and hope was found in a powdered drink. THIS MEDICATION HAS BEEN LIFE-CHANGING FOR ME.

It has given me enough bulk by absorbing water that I have more consistent bowel movements. Considering my state of mind at the time, it may have very well saved my life.

What I discovered - second

Another dietary supplement for GI health has helped me tremendously. It is a combination of probiotics and prebiotics. So, what is the difference between the two, and what is the synergistic benefit of taking both?

Probiotics	**Prebiotics**
Live microorganisms	Are not live organisms

Probiotics (cont'd.)	**Prebiotics**
"Good bacteria"	Helps good bacteria grow
Feed off of prebiotics	A food source for probiotics

When taken together in correct proportions, the pro and prebiotics help maintain the GI tract and boost our immune system. I found that taking one of these per day has significantly helped my digestive issues. Most of the time, I even have a few minutes of a pre-poop warning.

What I discovered - third

My booty washer!

I purchased a bidet seat for my bathroom. This was the best money (about $300) I've ever spent. It has a nice warm seat along with a selection of wash cycles. I can choose lukewarm water, warm water, or very warm water. There are options for a gentle washing or a more vigorous cleansing for messy occasions. There's a steady stream or a side-to-side water pulse. But wait! There's more! I can get my booty blow-dried, too. It's the ultimate in cleanliness. The best part, though? When I have to endure two-day colonoscopy preps, I save so much toilet paper. And I'm not nearly as raw. This big ol' booty almost smiles.

What I discovered – fourth

I bought a travel toilet for my car! To the untrained eye (for lack of a better word), it appears to be a small leather ottoman — the top lifts off to reveal a lightly padded ring (seat). The bottom of the "ottoman" is lined with a bathroom trash bag. My friend, Marie, recommended putting a couple cups of clumping cat litter into

the bottom of the bag, just in case it couldn't be disposed of quickly. I even have a mock curtain to give me a bit of privacy if needed. Squat, wipe, and go!

What I did for myself - an act of desperation

There came a time after I'd been in so many desperately mortifying situations and denied bathroom access to non-public restrooms that I decided to use the Cancer card. I had business card size information cards printed to explain why I needed access to their restroom even though they may not typically allow the public to use them.

Only twice in the past ten years was I turned down after presenting this card. The first time was in a national chain Christmas store. Upon politely asking if I could use the restroom, the cashier barked that they have no public restrooms and I'd have to go next door to another establishment. I ran across the street to a fast-food restaurant, and when I was finished, I marched my depleted self back to the store, demanding to see the manager. Conveniently, the cashier who earlier denied me said he went to the bank.

"I. WILL. WAIT." I growled back at her with my eyes narrowing.

Not happy with my response, she said he would likely not return for the day.

"Of course, he won't," I added snidely and with rolling eyes. "Here. Do something for me. Do you see this card? Make me a Xerox copy, but blow it up to about 250% and do the same for the other side."

She went into a closed-door room, and moments later, she returned with the original card and the copy. Taking the card, I thanked her and said (loud enough for other customers to hear), "When your manager opens up the door, give him/her this (the copy) and make sure he reads it. It will explain to him or her that some individuals do have medical issues requiring a bit of compassion and understanding due to circumstances such as cancer radiation treatments. Not everyone wants convenience. It can be NECESSARY to use the nearest facility." I threw the copies at her, and as I walked out the door, I assured her I would be calling their corporate office.

Cancer. A Journey Of A Thousand Miles.

Additional help

When traveling:

There's an app called *FLUSH.* No matter your current location or future travel destination, this app is valuable for locating public restrooms. Some are even listed as "requires key," "requires a fee," or "disabled access." Genius! It even allows you to add a toilet location so other app users will know.

Other Available Treatments for Incontinence:
Kegel Exercises – pelvic floor exercises
Biofeedback – electrical patches monitor muscle
strength. Therapy is planned accordingly.
Bulking Agents – nonabsorbable injections
Sacral Nerve Stimulation – implantation of a small
device that sends electrical impulses, much
like a pacemaker does for the heart. The stimulated
nerve regulates the bladder or bowel.
Medication – different ones for urinary/fecal

I MISS MY MIND

I'm not going to lie; there were times when I thought I had completely lost my mind. There was a complete absence of a thought or a word. Some have called this phenomenon a "brain fog," or a "chemo fog," or "mental clouding." I called it the "this-is-really-pissing-me-off-right-now-because-my-brain-was-the-only-good-part-of-me-left-FOG"! The rest of me was being destroyed by chemo and radiation, and now my mind was being attacked. NOOOOO! This stops now!

If it was only that easy.

According to some healthcare studies, chemo brain, despite the name, isn't confirmed to be only caused by chemotherapy. In one study, 25-30 percent of patients began having cognitive issues before starting their chemotherapy treatment.

So, if chemo brain can potentially begin before chemo, then what else could cause the symptoms?

- Hormone therapy
- Radiation treatment
- Lack of sleep (stress from the diagnosis)
- Depression
- Chemical changes within the body
- Cancer within the brain
- Genetic susceptibility to chemobrain
- Other cancer treatments [3]

---

3. Mayo Clinical Staff. "Chemo Brain." Pruthi, Sandhya, et al, 09 Feb 2023 www.mayoclinic.org/diseases-conditions/chemo-brain/symptoms-causes/syc-20351060, Accessed 18 Feb 2024

Some people say that chemo brain isn't even real. Maybe, these are people who went through treatment and were in the 25 percent minority who didn't experience mental clarity problems.

Below are typical symptoms; each presented to me at some point. I struggled a lot.

- Being unusually disorganized (this really messed with my emotional health because I despise inorganization)

- Confusion and difficulty concentrating

- Trouble finding the right word and mental fogginess
- Struggling to multitask and to learn new skills

- Short attention span or short-term memory problems

- Taking longer than usual to complete routine tasks

- Trouble with verbal memory, such as remembering a conversation

- Trouble with visual memory, such as recalling an image or list of words

Symptoms and their duration differ among individuals, and this side effect can persist from a few months to several years after the treatment concludes.

Practices that helped me to focus on daily tasks

1.   My biggest struggle was trying to follow simple directions. A recipe, for example. It would be necessary to read, reread, and read again (maybe several more times) before I could do that simple task. I ordered the home-delivery meal kits to make life a bit less chaotic. From the outside looking in, some family members thought, "Must be nice" or "She wants groceries delivered so she doesn't have to go shopping because she is spoiled." The directions with the kits were broken down and separated into smaller, more manageable sections for comprehension. That was a huge benefit.

Although I still read and reread, I could handle short sections to get it done. I received four meals every other week.

We ate out. We ate out a lot. Both the meal kits and eating out became costly in the long term. So, mealtime became extraordinarily simple. Boring. One night, it could be a frozen pizza. The next night, we might have had French fries. On a particularly ambitious day, soup and sandwiches. I am embarrassed and ashamed to admit that.

As time passed and my stamina increased, I began planning and fixing "real meals." What a sense of accomplishment I felt. My method for success was to write down everything I planned to fix. I'd write the combined prep and cook time from the first item. To the left of the dish name, I'd write down the time that item needed to be started. For each food in the meal, I would do this. To ensure I wouldn't lose focus, I'd promptly set a timer on my phone for each item's start time. While this may seem juvenile, it was highly effective, and I gained the confidence to push forward.

2.   When I needed to make a telephone call and became fearful of sounding stupid because I could lose my train of thought or not recall a particular word, I would faithfully make notes to cover all I needed to address. I knew I wasn't stupid. I also knew how ridiculously judgmental and impatient people can be. For doctors' visits, I entered notes or questions into my phone. Things got done, whatever it took.

3.   I had a short attention span. The only thing I could think of to help me focus intently on one thing was to do something requiring me to concentrate fully on a task. Learning to paint was my project of choice. I, admittedly, stumbled upon this revelation when setting up my bathroom or a two-day colonoscopy prep. You see, I needed something to do in there. Dragging my easel, tubes of acrylic paints, and my box of brushes, I readied myself to learn. My hope was two-fold: I would learn a craft and pass the time in a more tolerable way. YouTube provided me with many beginner paint options, and I happily chose a fall scene and adjusted the easel's height. After a coat of gesso, I began the project.

I followed along, trying to recreate what I watched in the video. Watch. Pause the video. Paint. Pause. Evaluate. And then, watch, paint, pause, evaluate, rewind, rewatch, rewatch, paint, repaint, pause, and evaluate. By the end of the day, it was stare, paint,  poop, paint, poop, rewind, poop, poop, and so on. The result was not a masterpiece; it was, however, a success in thought redirection.

4.　　Other mental acuity issues, where I didn't feel as sharp as I did before treatment, led me to begin doing puzzles: crossword puzzles, word find puzzles, sudoku, and brain teasers – anything I thought would be brain stimulating. I have no idea if these were beneficial, but I continue to do them today for the challenge alone.

NOW A LYMPHIE

Lymphedema presented itself about three months post-treatment. Everything else had been ongoing or had presented later.

Whenever radiation damages the lymph nodes and disrupts the flow of lymph fluids, swelling occurs in the arms or legs. This swelling is known as lymphedema.

The lymph nodes act as fluid-filtering centers. Excess fluid throughout the body is sent to the lymph nodes, and impurities are filtered out before the fluid is sent back into the circulatory system. Lymphocytes, a type of white blood cell, attack and destroy bacteria and other foreign substances inside the node.

The fluid in the lymphatic system is called lymph fluid. There aren't any red blood cells in the lymph fluid. Lymph is the blood's plasma (watery fluid containing white blood cells).

In the cardiovascular system, the heart pumps blood through the body. In the lymphovascular system, there is no pumping mechanism. Our muscles move lymph fluid toward the heart. But if the fluid isn't moving as it should be, it doesn't flow back to the heart, and that causes fluid buildup, known as edema. Edema of lymph fluid is lymphedema.

There are those who specialize in treating this condition. When searching for a practitioner, look for a Certified Lymphedema Therapist (CLT). They have been specifically trained in all aspects of lymphedema therapy, compression, and skin care. The oncology center had a lymph specialist, and she was terrific. She carefully measured my right thigh, calf, and ankle and then did the same with my left leg. She determined I would be best suited for medium-sized stockings with 20-30 mmHg. That number is the amount of compression in millimeters of Mercury, as shown on a blood pressure cuff. The amount of compression the stockings would provide would be like pumping a blood pressure cuff until the needle is at 25. That would mean 25 mmHg (millimeters of mercury) of compression on my legs at all times. That's the clinical picture.

When I ordered my stockings, I was happy to learn that there were knee highs, thigh highs, waist highs, somewhat sheer options, color choices, prints, and toeless ones. For more severe lymphedema, there are wraps, wraps with compression pumps, and wraps for arms, legs, feet, head, and torso. I preferred the toe-less stockings.

There were so many guidelines to be aware of, and I needed to make lifestyle changes as well as be very careful not to cut myself or get any wounds. When I took a nasty fall onto the concrete, I obtained a fairly deep gash on my shin. It took seem-ingly forever to heal, and I'd frequently feel blood running down my leg. However, it wasn't the normal red blood I had expected to see. It was a very slightly blood-tinged, cloudy, and viscous lymph fluid. With lymphedema, healing is a slower process, and there is an increased risk of infection.

Lifestyle changes that I made:

New option that I chose	*Why?*
Switched to electric shaver	*Prone to infection; if cut*
No hot tubs, saunas, hot showers	*Increased swelling*
No bare feet outside	*Risk of breaking open any cracks in the skin*

No tight jewelry, shoes, or clothing	*Irritation – skin could break*
Use sunscreen and bug-repellent	*Infection-prone*
Moisturize skin (no alcohol, fragrances, dyes, mineral oil) or petroleum	*Low-pH products are the best*

Also: When traveling, stand up every two hours.

There is some controversy as to whether this is needed. I err on the side of caution, wear my compression garments, and try to move as much as possible. If on a long flight, doing toe and heel raises seems to help.

I completed my radiation treatment in late April, but my lymphedema did not present until late July. There were some workdays when I couldn't even conform to my left shoe, which was worse than my right. Since I left my career, the swelling has dramatically improved. Still, when it's hot outside and I spend long periods on my feet, my legs swell and become painful. The skin appears shiny due to the tight stretching, and the lymphedema causes redness, heat, and pitting.

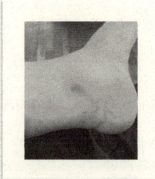

PITTING LYMPHEDEMA

SEX IS A PAIN

(Content warning:
Mildly graphic and written with poignancy)

This is not a sexual article. It's a clinical article (as clinical as I can make it). I'm putting this in here because it's another topic that should be discussed.

Sex is a pain. It hurts. Not hurt like a bee sting. It hurt like razors slicing through and cross-wise shredding the rawness of my innermost parts until flesh fragments were delivered. And then pour acetone on that. Yeh. That's pretty accurate.

Pelvic radiation is hard on your body. Everything that gets radiated is damaged. Lymph nodes, rectal area, everything. And, although I didn't know it until my husband and I tried sex, my vaginal canal had narrowed and shortened.

It's a condition called *vaginal stenosis*. The first attempt at penetration was excruciating. I honestly didn't think I would ever want to have sex again. Next time, the same thing. Horrid pain. Lubricants did not help at all. It was a demanding and straightforward dichotomy because I loved sex. With it came shame, feelings of being less than, and also fears of being a disappointment to my newlywed husband.

But, with the patience of a saint, Paul started researching. He learned that this is a common problem after pelvic radiation AND some chemotherapies. He also learned that there are devices designed specifically for this problem. They are vaginal dilators.

dilators. (No one told me about this. Not my oncologist, not the radiation oncologist, absolutely no one!)

These devices are not dildos. They are not vibrators. **Dilators**. Dilators are in graduated sizes and are designed to stretch the vaginal walls.

This is how they're to be used:

Start with the smallest size, <u>just in case</u>, and attach it to the base. Liberally apply a water-based lubricant (such as K-Y jelly) to the dilator. Lie down on a bed, face up, and follow the directions that accompany the kit. If you have no pain, go to the next size, repeating the steps.

If the vagina is too tight to insert it fully, hold the dilator still and try to contract your pelvic muscles. Tighten and release.

Tighten and release. Continue this until the dilator can be fully inserted.

When the dilator is in, keep it there for five to ten minutes. (You may need to hold it inside to keep it from being pushed out.) Remove the dilator and wash it with mild soap and water. Do this process three times per week. I never did get  comfortable using the inflexible ones. I did, however, find and love these: These are called Cool Water Cones! Although they're made of mostly water, they can be reused for up to a month. They were designed by a scientist whose wife was going through painful pelvic radiation treatments. They feel like a jelly substance and are cool going in. It's much more "burn" friendly, in my opinion. The company recommends using them twice weekly. They are available online at CMTmedical.com.

Another tip:

It will also help to try different sex positions. I found that being on top gave me more control, and that was a benefit physically AND emotionally. The fear of the pain took its toll on my emotions. I first had to learn to relax emotionally and then physically. Things are finally better now. I don't believe I'll ever be back to one hundred percent, but I'm grateful. I only wish I had known this information beforehand.

Other available options:

- Your physician may recommend estrogen cream to soothe the tender vaginal walls and to help with dryness.

- There are gel packs (similar to a feminine pad) that can be put into your underwear for direct warm or cool soothing treatment.

- Over-the-counter vaginal lubricants

Remember to be patient with yourself. Talk to your partner openly about the internal damage that occurred as a result of radiation and chemo. The treatment saved our lives, not our vajayjays.

I HATE YOU, AND YOU, AND YOU

(Content warning – PTSD, PTED, Emotional Anger)

One of the fiercest battles that I fought was within myself. Most people have heard of PTSD (post-traumatic stress disorder). My response to the trauma was more of bitterness. I did not have nightmares or flashbacks of trauma, but instead, I had intense feelings of resentment and bitterness because of what the treatments had done to my body. When this type of anger and negativity affects day-to-day living, it is known as Post Traumatic Embitterment Disorder (PTED).

This persistent negative outlook affected all my relationships. I wasn't angry that cancer tried to kill me. I wasn't enraged at God. However, I was so angry at all the collateral damage I was left with. I hated that I was a vulnerable shell of who I used to be. I wanted to be left alone. No one understood anyway. How could they? That was inconsequential, though. I despised everyone for their lack of understanding and knowledge. Yes, that's irrational! And you can't reason with someone incapable of reasoning at the moment.

It was a long crippling season for me. For over three years, I diligently worked on modifying MY perspective. I could work toward educating others, but, I could not change their point of view until I corrected mine. So, I focused on empathy toward the onlookers of my circumstances, finding acceptance of my own emotions, and searching for the inner peace I once had, which brought me to a place of emotional healing. It was extensive work, but the alternative was dismal. Imagine a life of anger. From the moment my eyes were opened in the mornings, the ugliest and fiercest anger consumed me. My target was whoever stood before me. I had to sit face to face with the bitterness that stemmed from frustration, insecurities, and feelings of being overwhelmed. They had manifested as anger directed at random and unrelated triggers.

Peripheral Neuropathy and ruling out RILP

RILP is Radiation Induced Lumbosacral Plexopathy. This is a severe condition caused by pelvic radiation. It is rare, disabling, and without a cure. The radiation damages the lower (lumbar) spine and sacral portion of the pelvis. A plexus is a bundle of nerves. If these nerves have been damaged by irradiation, a wide range of symptoms may present. Leg pain, weakness, tingling, foot drop, and even paralysis. The symptoms can be treated, but the RILP won't go away.

My feet began to feel tingly and heavy; it was necessary to see a neurologist to discern what was happening. There were also a couple of episodes where my right foot would cramp terribly, and the toes would draw upward toward the shin. This occurred while driving, and it was disabling. I accelerated and braked with my right foot. Of course, I could drive with both feet and brake with the left, but the right foot and lower leg were so drawn up that I had to lift it with both hands to release acceleration or push down on my knee to press the accelerator. I couldn't steer when both hands were lifting or pushing my leg. I thought I was going to die in a motor vehicle crash that day. With a grimaced face of agony and confusion, I managed to press the hazard lights. Fully aware I was all over the road at vastly varying speeds, I did my best to push and pull that leg to get me the rest of the way to work. I somewhat steered with my left elbow. The right leg was immobilized.

I nearly fell when I arrived at work because my toes were still drawn. Over the next twenty minutes, the foot relaxed a little at a time, and the soreness lingered for twenty-four hours.

The neurologist had an opening the following week. That appointment was for a consultation and the outcome was that I would return for some testing to diagnose me better.

Diagnosis by testing (to rule out or confirm)

- Nerve Conduction Study

  Purpose - It was to see if my nerves were as "quick" as they should be and if there was any nerve "death."

  Procedure - Dr. Schwartz put little electrodes on my feet. He used a handheld device that looked like an electric cattle prod and pushed it into my leg at the location of a nerve. An electric current was sent through the device to stimulate that nerve. A computer measured how fast the current traveled and how long it took for my feet to recognize it (by my feet jerking). It wasn't painful but just a "zapping" sensation. At the point when he hit the one inside my right ankle, that was quite uncomfortable.

  "Apparently, that one is entrapped," Dr. Schwartz said.

  One zap, and it burned like fire. It hurt. He touched the skin with his hand, and it seared like fire. I shed a couple tears and reached for Paul's hand. The rest of the testing was a piece of cake compared to that.

- EMG (Electromyography)

Purpose - This test was for muscle (myo means muscle) instead of nerve.

Procedure - This time, Dr. Schwartz stuck very thin needles (again attached to some current) into my muscles and had me move my feet around. The computer recorded the muscular activity (I could hear it, too!). The needles hurt way less than I anticipated. I was expecting something much worse.

Diagnosis - In the end, he said that I do have some chronic bilateral neuropathy. That means nerve pain that is slowly progressing on both sides.

He wouldn't (or couldn't) commit to saying it is 100 percent caused by the radiation, but he did say that IF that is the case, it will continue to get worse, and there's "no cure." He did add that usually, neuropathy of the extremities is more likely to be caused by chemotherapy than radiation.

Dr. Schwartz made an unexpected observation during this visit. During the physical exam, he noticed that the last four toes would curl down on each foot, as they should. Yet, none of them would flex upwards as they should. He didn't seem alarmed, but I was asked to do this repeatedly for several minutes as he would say, "Hmm" or "I see."

As I have researched this, there doesn't seem to be a definitive link between chemo or radiation and the lack of toe movement. This is likely claw toes forming. Sounds attractive, doesn't it? Just add it to my "freak of nature" list. I know, I know. You want to be me. <<laughing>>

Hair Today, Gone Tomorrow

As I described in a previous chapter, hair loss had a painfully profound impact on me. And I never grew it all back. Unfortunately, it's patchy, and my scalp is easily exposed enough to sunburn on the cloudiest days.

You may have heard that after chemo hair grows back with a different texture or color. Mine grew back about the same color, but I developed chemo curls. From everything that I have read, chemo curls are not usually permanent. I have had them for ten years now, so I will venture to say that mine will be permanent. Overachiever.

I shared the story about going to get my head shaved. Although I didn't bare head it, I was thin enough that my vanity took over, and I opted to go wig shopping.

After sitting on the mall bench for about fifteen minutes, trying to find the courage to go into the wig shop, "It'll be fun," I told myself. "Go in there and try on something funky and cute!" Anxiety barraged my mind, and tears welled up in the corners of my eyes. "I can't do it!" I desperately clung to Paul. He reminded me that it wasn't something I had to do, but if I wanted to, he'd be right beside me, and he knew I'd be proud of myself when I walked out. "C'mon, baby, I'm right beside you."

So onward, I marched, wide-eyed and visibly emotional.

I didn't make a purchase there, but I did try a few on. The lady salesperson, with a ridiculous amount of makeup (and hair), told us about a program where cancer patients could get a free wig. She provided the address. I think she didn't love the idea of someone sickly trying on her high-dollar wigs. I'm sure that wasn't the case, her demeanor was just so hoity-toity. I left feeling as bleak as when I had entered.

There was a wig shop at the cancer center. The wigs were gently used, and the woman there was phenomenal and welcoming. I was led to a private "try-on" area where I could feel free to be me. I did take home a wig from there.

Today, I use various methods to cover the thin spots where hair should be. I have purchased toppers; they are kind of like a toupee for women, colored fibers that I sprinkle on, or a colored scalp spray that conceals the bald patches. Women who color their hair also use the latter two to cover roots.

I would be negligent if I failed to mention the only advantage of hair loss. The loss of hair on my legs! That didn't all come back, either. I can go two weeks without shaving.

Hey, I'll look for that rainbow anywhere.

FATTY, FATTY; 2 BY 4

Fatty, fatty; two by four.

Can't fit through the kitchen door.

Just as wide as she is tall;

Don't look now, she ate it all!

I remember the first two sentences as a jump rope rhyme from my childhood. However, I don't recall the remaining lines, so I made them up.

My oncologist told me to eat calories because he wanted me to maintain my weight. For once, being overweight wasn't a bad thing. During treatments, I lost about fifteen pounds, and my biggest obstacle was that nearly every food made me nauseous—everything but carbs, that is. Potatoes, milkshakes, pasta, and bread were great. But a nice salad or meatloaf or casserole, nope. Before my diagnosis, I was eating cleanly. My friend Katie and I traded recipes and made smoothies for each other, taking turns every other day. Even my makeup was certified organic. I was on the highway to excellent health.

Oh, the irony.

If you'd asked me then, "Is there such a thing as a carb addiction?" I would've laughed you back to where you came from. "Just shut your mouth and make better choices! You're not unintelligent!" would've been my response.

I honestly think God has a sense of humor sometimes. I can almost hear Him chuckling at the absurdity of my know-it-all

167

thoughts as He allows me a hefty dose of carb addiction to learn from.

Any form of roughage tore me up and angered the diverticulosis. That's just perfect! <<sarcasm>> Greasy food and most meats were a no-go, and so were many vegetables, even cooked. Never a big fruit eater, bananas were my only faithful snacks. So, what did that leave me with? Carbs. And more carbs. Pasta, sandwiches (at least there was some protein), potatoes, rice, pretzels, etc.

After treatments, eating a salad without GI upset took about six or eight months. Unfortunately, they weren't as satisfying as they once were. I craved carbs. I craved them like a drug. The more I indulged, the more I wanted. I was likely killing my pancreas by working it overtime. The pancreas helps our body manage glucose by sending out insulin to recruit the sugar, using it for energy. If your body isn't using that insulin effectively or the pancreas isn't producing enough, diabetes comes into play. I am now a diabetic. I probably did this to myself by overworking my pancreas. I essentially caused it to burn out. It no longer works efficiently. That's not likely clinically correct, but regardless of how or why, diabetes is now residing on my list of ailments.

A Hot and Spicy Girl

Oh, for the love of everything hot and spicy. Have you ever been in one of those hot pepper stores in boutique malls

168

where you must sign a release to try their hottest of hot peppers? I was one of those girls. My son and I even ate ghost peppers on our breakfast potatoes and eggs. We were fearless! I mean our GI systems were. Haha.

And then came chemo.

I can no longer handle hot and spicy foods - not my mouth or gut. Jalapeños are the hottest peppers I can now tolerate. My GI system is now wimpy. It's shameful to the former me. There have been so many changes! Some massive, some small, all important to me.

Chapter 14

SURVIVOR'S GUILT

W hy me?

I don't mean "**why me**," like why did I have to go through cancer. But why me, like, why have I been able to survive (even thrive) when others have not?

I have had "survivor's guilt" from time to time. I use that term because it is one that most people recognize. I haven't had a sense of actual guilt but a strong sense of **awe and sadness**. It's been difficult to wrap my brain around why I'm now okay when so many others are fighting for their next breath. Some are young people. Some are friends with reoccurrences. Some are people I've never met. I'm affected by that. And, sometimes, the pain is very real for me when I hear the news of a new diagnosis, prognosis, or the end of a life.

I relive the same scenario:

I want to, but I shouldn't, but I want to. But I won't – ask God, *"Why?" I know that somehow, in the myriad of emotions, confusion, and pain,* there is a purpose. He has a purpose for everything. And me, little me down here on this little planet, in this little state, in this little town, does not need the answer to that question now.

Occasionally, upon hearing *"the news"* of another diagnosis, *I've* even had moments when part of me wishes that it was **ME** and not **them**. Because, in my eyes, so many of them (patients) have so much to give and so much life to live. I have lived my life (I'm in my sixties, but they are young adults — with very young children — fighting the fight). Little children are holding their parent's hands while hearing "you have cancer," and it just doesn't seem fair. Whatever "fair" is. I have raised my children. I have had a good life. And I'm not "afraid" to die.

Please understand that that DOES NOT mean I am ungrateful to be alive. **Quite the contrary!** As I've said before, I am living a more profound and richer quality of life now (after cancer). I know that through my blog, I have helped people. They've learned what to expect on this journey and that they are not alone. Some have shared with me that what I shared made a big difference in their lives. And that has made a difference in my own life.

Survivor's guilt is a post-treatment emotion. Post-treatment emotions can be overwhelming. It can become controlling. And if it gets to that point, counseling may be required to get through it. And there's no shame in that. And remember, our emotions are God-given.

I have listed below some of the emotions that I and many people have described experiencing:

Guilt (from the feeling of either surviving when others have not or because of thoughts of having done – or not done – something to have "caused" the cancer)

Uncertainty (of what life has in store for you from this point on)

Anger (because of how cancer or the treatments have impacted your life — you may have a new "normal" because of post-treatment sequelae)

Depression (patients are often just physically and emotionally exhausted from the stress of everything, and long-term depression requires treatment … medication helps get the chemicals back in balance, and you WILL feel better …. trust me on this one)

Anxiety (over how you now see yourself — for example, if you are left with lymphedema or incontinence issues)

Fear (that the cancer will reoccur)

Spiritual concerns (sometimes patients can begin thinking about their mortality for the very first time — talk with a family member, pastor, hospital clergy member, or a friend)

Emotional numbness (those who can't take anymore may emotionally shut down. If someone says they "can't feel," believe them. It's true, and it is something that needs to be addressed by a professional, so reach out and allow someone to help).

Some devices to help you get through the emotions mentioned above:

Talk (to family, other survivors, someone in your church, cancer support groups, etc.)

Journal (write down what you are feeling because it does help to put those feelings into words)

Find a creative outlet such as coloring or painting (it doesn't have to be a pretty painting, or maybe you could try making bracelets, rods, or lures. One of my favorites is blowing bubbles) Yes! All are very therapeutic!

Volunteer (this is something we are often reluctant to do whenever we are feeling emotional; however, it truly helps us to redirect our thoughts and will move the focus to help other people — and, in turn — survivors will sometimes be surprised that THEY are the one benefitting from the act of kindness)

So, when I have a "why me" moment, how do I handle it? Well, I have accepted that I may never know why. I do not understand why I am still here. Maybe it is to share my experience. Maybe there is a greater purpose ahead. The Bible says that there is a time to live and a time to die. That time has already been decided, and God's timing is perfect in all things.

When it comes to cancer and losing someone I care about, I'll never again say that he/she "lost" their battle with cancer (or that cancer "stole" that someone from me). I refuse to give it that power! I will say they fought the beast with all they had and did so with dignity until their last breath.

If I should have a recurrence, subsequent cancer, or any other disease for that matter, that's how I would like to be remembered. I will be going down fighting until my last breath.

I know that my perfect healing lies ahead when my life here is over.

Chapter 15

DON'T BE AFRAID; BELIEVE

···

I had no faith in myself to beat cancer. I'm not that strong. But I know someone who has enough strength for both of us. God. Please don't shut me down here. Allow me to share with you how I came to know God and how knowing Him has changed my life. My faith is primarily what got me through this journey. Because of the strength I found through prayer and fellowship with other believers, I want to share that with you. You may think I got sick and had a "come to Jesus" moment. No.

Although my parents had sent me to church as a little girl, I was involved with the youth group and choir in my teenage years and tried to give my heart to Jesus when I was about seventeen; I wasn't 100 percent committed. When BJ and I were dating, and things were getting pretty serious, hormones started taking over. I knew what we were about to do was "wrong," and I was scared anyway, so I resisted in the name of my newfound faith.

"I gave my heart to Jesus, and I'm thinking we shouldn't do this."

"I need to know that you mean what you say," he replied.

My brain translated those words into "If you love me, you will."

I was too naive, shy, and unsure of myself to entertain the notion. Jesus was pushed to the back burner, where He waited until my heart authentically caught fire. Until then, I lived for myself, making my own decisions and pretending that I had everything under control. I lost my virginity on a yellow and brown quilt in my parent's bedroom.

When I was with Harry, I realized I needed something outside of myself: a Higher Power. Upon waking one Sunday morning, I had an incredibly vivid, sensory dream. Harry and I were sitting outside on the porch one evening. It was a bit chilly and my legs felt the coldness of the concrete steps leading to the patio. I'd seen a shooting star and pointed it out to him. In the next moment, from the south, a small yet bright, reddish spherical light appeared in the sky. Harry said, "Looky there." Inquisitively, I asked him what it was. Only seconds later, it had become apparent that it was a rapidly growing fireball! A massive ball of fire was being hurled to the earth. My boys! I have to get to my boys! My mind was in complete panic and chaos. Harry had already whisked me to the basement. We were huddled up against the cinderblock walls. Within seconds, we could feel the earth shaking. I watched Harry's brown eyes turn nearly black as a deafening, intense rumble rolled over our home. We felt the burning heat on the basement's blocks and we moved away from the wall to avoid being blistered. It was so hot, indescribably so. Then suddenly, nothing. Quiet. Still. Cool. We said nothing to each other but slowly walked through the French doors to the outside to see the destruction. There was none. Harry wiped the moisture from his tattooed arms. The earth was damp and misty, and sunshine peeked through the mist. We smelled the freshness of budding green trees and beautiful fragrant flowers. Nothing was scorched—no trace of an ash. Everything was made new. People were walking somewhere, so Harry cradled my hand in his, and we followed the line until we got to a church. Our words were unspoken but were implicitly felt through mutual eye contact. All fell to their knees upon arrival. People were singing. People were praising God. I turned to my right and asked Harry, "Why would God save US?!" He couldn't respond.

Upon awakening from the dream that morning, I went to a little church close to home, and it seemed small enough that it might be welcoming to "someone like me." I arrived early and waited in the parking lot for a while. No one showed up. Hmmmmm. Wondering if the service hours had changed, I drove around for a while and then returned to the parking lot. No one. Not a single vehicle. Jeesh. It's time for plan B. As soon as I got back home, I searched the phone book. Dial, DIAL, D I A L ! "Oh. Hello. What time does your service start? And, what attire is appropriate - I'm asking because the last church I went to was with a bunch of people who seemed to be trying to outdo each other with what they were wearing." The lady replied gently,

"11:00 a.m. and come as you are – we emphasize the message, not the wardrobe".

"I'll be there!" I said. I had ten minutes before the service began, so I hurried out the door. I arrived out of breath and looked a bit disheveled but was warmly welcomed by a sweet and seemingly genuine lady. "Hi", she said, smiling. "I'm Pastor Nancy, and I believe I just spoke with you on the phone." I acknowledged that I was, indeed, the one. We both had a little chuckle. She gave me a welcome pack and walked me into the sanctuary, introducing me to a lady sitting near the back on the left-hand side. Her name was Naomi, and she took me under her wing for the morning.

Now, here's a little bit of a freaky but incredible story. I only say freaky because it freaked me out at the moment. I had no Bible. I hadn't even opened one in a shamefully long time. Things were going along like church services do, and the Pastor asked the congregation to turn to a specific chapter and verse in the Bible. I suppose it would've seemed rude to my new acquaintance, Naomi, had I crawled under the pew or suddenly, at that very moment, desperately pleaded for a restroom. I did neither. Bewildered, I reached for one of the pew Bibles. I had no idea where to turn in that Bible. I knew there was an Old and New Testament; however, the book I was supposed to be turning to could've been in the Beatitudes for all I knew. Palms sweating, I quickly glanced over to Naomi to get some indication of front or back. My perception was that it was less than halfway through. Before Psalms. (Pretty good plan, eh?!) Pretending to be familiar with the pages I held before me, I opened to a starting point. Checking to see if there might be something I recognized, I was stunned to see I was already on the exact page — book, chapter, and verse. Freaky, I tell you. I think God Himself had an Angel turn that page for me as a sign saying, "I'm glad you're here."

I began attending that little church pretty faithfully. After a while, I even joined the Sunday school class. Those people were really friendly, joyful, and sincere. They treated me like I had been part of their group for years.

During the week, I was working toward a bachelor's degree at a nearby university. A hyper-enthusiastic woman about my age named Anita was in a couple of my classes. One day in the library, she shared a heart-wrenching story with me. She was a widow. She and her darling husband had been on their routine morning jog, and he collapsed onto the park's pavement, clutching his chest. Not long after, he died. Tearfully, I asked how it was that she exuded joy. I mean, this woman should be in a very dark place by all rights, but she's walking sunshine. Anita told me of her love of God and how He has continued to sustain her. She introduced me to a song entitled "I Can Only Imagine," and her bright, sunshiny eyes glistened through tears of praise. I was in awe of her spirit. There was "something" about her.

The following Tuesday, she invited me to a small women's Bible study she had been attending. Gracefully, I declinclined. If I were in a whole room full of all that sunshine and happiness, I'd likely puke (I mean, I'd probably put a damper on things). When the following Tuesday rolled around, she asked me again. I made up some excuse. And so it went for the next few weeks, each time she looked into my heart with those gentle yet soulful blue eyes full of joy. Finally, as much as I genuinely did like Anita, it became evident that I would either have to be blunt and risk hurting her feelings or accept her invitation. I chose the latter. Just to shut her up, I'd go one time.

These women were oozing with peace. I'd never seen anything like it. They prayed, and Kendra taught a lesson, relating it to life in the present. They shared and chatted, and there wasn't any "in-your-face-holier-than-thou" stuff. I didn't want to go home! Eagerly, I awaited the following Tuesday when Anita asked me if I'd like to join her. With all the restraint I could muster, I toned down my enthusiastic "Heck yeh" to "I'd love to, thank you." Hmmm, something inside me was changing.

A couple of months later, on Tuesday, June 19, 2001, I crawled into bed after that night's Bible study and prayed for God to give me whatever they had. I told Him that I didn't want to do life on my own anymore because I kept screwing it up. And I said to Him that I wanted and needed Jesus to come into my heart, to forgive me, and to please save me from the horrible person I was. I felt tears spilling onto my pillow. I wanted to be a better me. A better mom. A better companion. I wanted to be whoever He designed me to be.

182

And that's precisely what happened. I felt peace in a very real and unmistakable way. I knew He was with me, and He knew I was being real that time. I had a fire in my heart, and it was burning brightly. Like a sponge, I absorbed as much as I could of God's Word. I listened to radio broadcasts and continued to learn from Kendra's Bible study. When I had the opportunity, I was baptized and joined the church.

On September 11th, 2001, I had a sleep study scheduled in the next county. I was participating in my blood bank clinical rotation at River Valley Medical Center when our country was terrorized. Although an hour and a half from my sons, they were all I could think of. I have to get to them. I have to be with them. I want to be with them!

As families across America were doing, I, too, called my loved ones.

After my rotation ended at 4:00 p.m., my brain was still in a web of tangled thoughts. Should I go to Fairfield? There's nothing I can do once I get there. Would my presence calm them or make them more anxious? Should I cancel my sleep study? I wonder what everyone else is going to do. Everything was so incredibly uncertain.

When I arrived at home, I asked Harry for his opinion. He chuckled and said, "Well, I don't think anyone will target the Unity Hospital! Go."

Anita had called, and we were still having Bible study. We gathered and earnestly prayed for our country.

The skies were dark, and the cumulus clouds seemed very low when I left Bible study for the hospital. I prayed over and over again. "God, should I go? Am I supposed to go?" After my umpteenth prayerful pleading, I heard a quiet voice say, "It's okay — go." This voice was not a voice I recognized. It wasn't an audible voice that someone else in the car would've heard. However, I listened to that voice loudly and clearly as if it was audible.

Moreover, I had sublime peace following. Everything was fine, and I slept like a baby during the study.

Two months later, I had to have a mass removed from my lower left lung. My surgeon, Dr. Greene, was a man of great girth and personality with gray eyes that smiled on their own. He maintained a voice of composure as he told me, "If it walks like a duck and quacks like a duck — It's probably a duck." I'm not sure whether the change in his eyes was sympathy or empathy, as he revealed to me a dense mass on my CT scan. He explained, and I could clearly see, that the mass had the clinical characteristics of malignancy. I wasn't fearful or apprehensive about anything.

On the scheduled day, at 6:02 am, I arrived to be prepped. Ironically, Harry had been taken to another hospital with a severe episode of pancreatitis; I began to "feel" alone. I had peace once again before I'd been wheeled to the OR. I felt an unexplainable peace. A peace that "I" shouldn't have had. I should've been a bundle of nerves, yet I was sublimely calm. Until I looked into Harry's eyes, that is. I broke some at that point.

Please understand that I am not always calm; I do lose my temper. I do transgress. I have wanted to punch someone in the face multiple times. I am not perfect. I am an imperfect human who believes in and loves God.

I am an imperfect human who desires to be forgiven for messing up daily. I'm also a flawed human who wants to offer help to others who are struggling and to love all people simply because they are. I am an imperfect human who wants God's best for me. If I tell you I pray for you, I do. I can confidently say that because I do that immediately or within the next few minutes. It is a privilege to be able to approach the throne of the Almighty to pray on behalf of another "When we trust in Him, we're free to say whatever needs to be said, bold to go wherever we need to go." – Ephesians 3.12 [4]

He does hear us, "When you call on Me, when you come and pray to Me, I'll listen." – Jeremiah 29.12 [5]

We, as humans, don't always like how He answers us. Sometimes, He answers in the exact way we hope He will.

Other times, He answers with a "no" because we ask with the wrong motives. "Because you know you'd be asking for what you have no right to. You're spoiled children, each wanting your own way." – James 4.3 [6]

---

4.   The Message Bible. Peterson, Eugene H., NavPress, 2002.
5.   The Message Bible.
6.   The Message Bible.

He may say "no" because we don't believe. Jesus was matter-of-fact: "Yes – and if you embrace this kingdom life and don't doubt God, you'll not only do minor feats like I did to the fig tree, but also triumph over huge obstacles. This mountain, for instance, you'll tell, 'Go jump in the lake,' and it will jump. Absolutely everything, ranging from small to large, as you make it a part of your believing prayer, gets included as you lay hold of God. Ask boldly, believingly, without a second thought." [7] – Mathew 21:21-22.

And, sometimes, when it seems like He doesn't answer or doesn't hear us, He is waiting because maybe He has something BETTER in mind. Everything God does and is, is love. "I know what I'm doing. I have it all planned out – plans to take care of you, not abandon you, plans to give you the future you hope for." – Jer. 29.11 [8] and, since He doesn't live in a time continuum like we do (minutes, days, weeks, etc.), waiting seems like an eternity. We, in our impatience, are tempted to skip God (He said "no" after all) and fast forward with our self-devised plan. I have done this. Then, curiously, when it didn't work out, cried out, "God! Help!!"

My son put it best when he said, "An imperfect Christian is not a hypocrite, but human."

---

7.   The Message Bible.
8.   The Message Bible.

I learned more about the sacrifice that Jesus made. Why was it so important? The reason He had to come to earth was to live as mankind does, to tell the people about His Father in Heaven, to make disciples of ordinary, messed-up people, and to teach them. He healed the sick, forgave sins, and was love personified. He suffered an atrocious scourging and death to take on (thereby absolving) every single sin of every single person – past, present, and FUTURE. Yes. When He died, He already knew that I would need forgiveness. And without that forgiveness and salvation, I would spend an eternity with unmeasurable pain and torment.

In the Old Testament, it was customary for the people to offer up a spotless sacrifice, such as a lamb, to atone for the people's sins. When Jesus came, he was sinless, perfect. He willingly went to the cross to become a sacrifice for every sin of mankind. He was the perfect, spotless sacrifice. There is no need to sacrifice animals anymore. Jesus did it for all of us ahead of time.

I believe in a God that I can't see. Why? Because I believe what the Bible says and I've seen the difference that God has made in my life. The Bible is not a storybook written by a bunch of random, contradictory people. It's not a "religious" book. The Bible is the God-breathed Word. Now, I know some people say God didn't write it; people did. That's true, but that isn't the truth in its entirety. Those who wrote down the scriptures did so as historical documentation of the Hebrew/Jewish people, their relationship with God, and then later, the life, teachings, and interactions with

Jesus. I believe God breathed these writings into His people. A collaboration, if you will. For instance, if my husband wrote this book based on his observations, his relationship with me, and conversations and situations he witnessed, he could write it with my influence/inspiration. It may be a good book, but it wouldn't last forever. There would be errors and inaccuracies. I wouldn't be around forever to ensure nothing would be added, subtracted, or changed. The Bible was documented, translated into multiple languages, and likely argued over what books should be contained within. Some books contain (Old Testament) law; others are primarily history. There are books of poetry/music, letters addressed to the people, books of prophecy, and the gospels. There is documentation of witness's accounts of changed lives. All of the books are still relevant, and there are no contradictions. What many people think of as a contradiction is simply the law prior to Christ's coming (the Old Testament) and His Covenant with the people as was sealed by His death and Resurrection (the New Testament). There have been home fires that destroyed everything to the ground except for the Holy Bible, which remained intact and unburned by flames. The only thing in the home that survived. Isn't that profound? My book certainly doesn't have that anointing over it.

I'd like to briefly address some frequently asked questions about the nature of the God I believe in.

FAQs:

God IS: Perfect and Holy

Q. If He is so perfect and Holy, why did He die a brutal death? Why didn't he call a legion of angels to rescue Him?

A. It is true that Jesus has all of Heaven at His beck and call. He did not, however, need to be rescued. He wasn't a victim. He willingly gave His life on our behalf and often alluded to the time when His hour would come. When it did, He willingly and lovingly went to that cross — for me and you.

"I freely lay down my life. And so, I am free to take it up again. No one takes it from me. I lay it down of my own free will. I have the right to lay it down; I also have the right to take it up again. I received this authority personally from my Father." – John 10:18[9]

God is: The only One who can (and does) love us unconditionally

Q. How could He possibly love me without Judgement after everything I've done?   You don't know what all I've done.

A. God doesn't care what we've done if we sincerely ask for forgiveness, He forgives them. He says,

---

9.   The Message Bible

Cancer. A Journey of a Thousand Miles.

"They'll get to know me by being kindly forgiven, with the slate of their sins forever wiped clean." – Hebrews 8:12 [10]

God is: A triune God (Father, Son – Jesus, and Holy Spirit)

Q. How can God be three things at one time, and all of them be deities?

A. *I don't know, but I know that He Is. The best analogy I can come up with is to look at 2-hydrogen atoms and one oxygen atom. H_2O.*

H_2O is water.

H_2O is also steam/vapor.

H_2O is also ice.

These forms are the same (2-hydrogens and 1-oxygen), yet they are distinctly different.

God is: All-knowing

Q. Well, if He knows everything, why do I have to pray, and why doesn't He stop me from making bad decisions?

---

10. The Message Bible

A. He is a loving God who wants to hear from and communicate with His creation (us, His children). Just as we love hearing from our children, He loves hearing from us, and He tells us that.

"This is eternal life, that they may know You, the only true God, and Jesus Christ whom You have sent." – John 17:3 [11]

t interfere with our decision-making because He gave us free will. He won't force us to "do right," and He won't make us choose Him. The apostle Paul told this to the Galatians (New Testament).

"My friends, you were chosen to be free. So don't use your freedom as an excuse to do anything you want. Use it as an opportunity to serve each other with love." – Galatians 5:13 [12]

Adam and Eve had free will. There was ONE tree that they were told not to eat from. They partook. They chose to turn from God's Will.

God is: Everywhere at all times

Q. Can you prove that? No one can be everywhere at the same time.

---

11. The Message Bible
12 . The Message Bible

Cancer. A Journey of a Thousand Miles.

A. God doesn't live in time and space as we do. He isn't confined by parameters that only our minds can understand. He tells us that.

"Am I not a God near at hand" – God's Decree – "and not a God far off? Can anyone hide out in a corner where I can't see him?" GOD's Decree. "Am I not present everywhere, whether seen or unseen?" GOD's Decree. – Jeremiah 23:23-24 [13]

God is: Just (fair and consistent)

Q. How is it fair that some people live in poverty while others do not? And how is it fair that children get cancer? Or that. . .

A. Just (fair and consistent) is kind and loving. He corrects us when we are wrong, just as we do with our children. Children must be taught what is good because, even as babies, we are inherently bad (sinful). We don't even need to commit a sin to be considered a sinner. It's simply part of who we are as humans. And as heart-wrenching as it is to see children (or any loved one) sick, the sickness isn't a consequence of sin.

The bottom line:

It doesn't matter what we've done in the past. And it does not matter how "good" of a person we think we are now, or how

---

13. The Message Bible

much we give to charity or help at the local food bank. It doesn't matter if we struggle with addiction, if we have been abusive, or if we feel as if we fail at everything. It doesn't matter if our "good deeds" outnumber our "bad deeds." The only thing that matters is our relationship with God—believing in and accepting Him. When we take Jesus into our lives, we get a clean slate. We get a clean slate every day. It's that easy. It really is!

Look, I feel like I am the biggest sinner on the face of the earth. I'm not even kidding. I had a horrendously ugly past because I chose to sin from an early age. I knew right from wrong. I chose wrong. I chose to sin—a lot. I wanted to be my boss and not submit to anyone or anything. I hurt myself and a lot of other people. And I have taken all that garbage to my God and cried out for forgiveness. In His love and mercy, He forgave ALL OF IT. So, when I became sick, even if I was going to die, I still knew that I was going to be OKAY. Because I know, with 100 percent certainty, that I will be in Heaven when I die. I was sincere, God knew it, He forgave all my sin – past, present and future.

So, what is SIN? Sin is anything that is outside of God's Will.

Here's the thing …. **if** we ask God to forgive us and honestly ask Him to change our lives by coming into our hearts, **He will**. We have to mean it. We can't fool the God of the universe. He knows our hearts. If we mean it and want to be forgiven and live a life with Christ in us, we will. Just talk to Him and tell Him that. Your life will change. For some, it's a significant and immediate change. For others, it's a gradual change. But either way, your life is going to change. You will be forgiven. You will spend eternity in Heaven.

My change was gradual. I started feeling bad when I did something that I knew was wrong. I wanted to do what was pleasing to God. I started talking to God more (praying), not just when I "needed" or "wanted" something, but for guidance for everyday things. Joy filled my heart. I have also learned that joy does not equal happiness. Joy is peace in your heart that comes from knowing that God (the Holy Spirit) lives within you. Happiness is different. Happiness is an expression of contentment, like when things are going to your satisfaction. I can have joy in my heart while at the same time crying my eyes out because a loved one is dying.

Having God in your life does not mean you will have a trouble-free life. Jesus himself was taunted and hated by many. I have been mocked, hated, and disrespected, but having God in your life will give you peace and strength during those times of trouble. I know because I have that. It's a peace that I can't even understand. It's awesome!

So, if you decide to have Jesus in your life, you need to talk to God. Talking to God is praying, and you don't have to use a bunch of "fancy Bible words" such as Thee, Thou, hast, Ye, and so forth. So, pray in your own words (with your whole heart), or you can even pray something like this:

"Dear God, thank you for hearing my prayer. I know that I'm not living the life you want for me. I am a sinner. I believe that the Bible is true and that Jesus died on the cross so that I can be forgiven of my sins and can go to heaven as if I have never sinned in my life. I want you to come into my heart to be my Lord and Savior and to change me. Please forgive me for all my sins against You. Fill the emptiness inside of me with your Holy Spirit. I thank you, as I believe this is being done. Amen."

That's it. Salvation is yours.

Now, I will add that just because you have "fire insurance" doesn't mean you don't need to protect your "house." You'll start wanting to "do better" when temptation comes to look for you. You'll want to do what you know is right. You won't be perfect; only Jesus is. But I assure you that your life will change in an amazing way!

I still mess up every day. I still have doubts and fears from time to time. I am certainly aware of it now, and I can correct that behavior, repent and ask forgiveness, and then move on. I'm not perfect, and I never will be. You won't be either. But we are forgiven. And there is freedom in that! God is so good; His Goodness and Mercy make all the difference in our lives.

(Content warning: death and violence)

In this world we live in today, anything could happen to any one of us at any given moment. There may not be time for a

"Hail Mary" prayer. There may not be moments before death. Think about this. My dad was killed instantly by a gunshot wound to the head while hunting. People are killed instantly by auto accidents. Young adults are being mowed down on campuses by rapid-fire automatic rifles. Heart attacks, seizures, comas, freak accidents, etc. There is no lifetime guarantee for time on earth.

Some may say that I am crazy and weak. That's fine. What have I lost when I die, and if it was for naught? Absolutely nothing. On the flip side, what if I am right? What if everything I shared is true? Then, I gained everything, and the only thing I lost was a one-way ticket to the pits of an agonizing fiery hell that is infinitely tortuous. Jesus, for the win! It has already been declared.

And, please don't think that you need to "clean yourself up" before coming to God or that you're not worthy of being in His Presence. He uses the "unusable, imperfect messes" that we are. The twelve disciples were all ordinary people with hang-ups and imperfections, just like me and you. They were morally and ethically flawed, regular. I'll show you:

Disciple	Character traits
Simon (Peter)	Impulsive and inconsistent
Andrew	Quiet, reserved

Disciple (cont'd.)	Character traits
James (John's brother)	Hot-headed and quick to judge
John (James' brother)	Hot-headed and egotistical
Philip	Seemed to have a little OCD
Bartholomew (Nathaniel)	Had some "local" prejudice
Matthew	Greedy, hated, despised
Thomas	Cynical and pessimistic
James ("the lesser")	Weak faith
Thaddeus (son of James)	Violent
Simon (the zealot)	Religious radical, unstable
Judas	A traitor, hypocrite and narcissist

They were each regular people with flaws whom Jesus used to impact the world positively. He wants to do the same with you and me. Think about how God used those misfit ragamuffins to change the world. He wants to do the same with the misfits of today.

I'm so glad to have been able to depend on His strength during my journey. So many people have told me how strong I was. The thing is, I wasn't strong. Not strong enough to do it on my own. But I know the One who is strong enough for both of us.

Cancer. A Journey of a Thousand Miles.

There is a verse in the New Testament, in the Book of Mark, which became my cancer verse throughout my illness. It says, "Don't worry; just have faith". – Mark 5:36b [14]

And that's precisely what I did.

---

[14] Bible, Contemporary English Version, American Bible Society, 1995

Chapter 16

WHAT CANCER TAUGHT ME

L ife . . . Available for a limited time only. Limit one (1) per person. Non-transferrable. Woven with the finest components available. Expiration date is subject to change without notice. Contents are fragile. Handle with care. Terms and conditions apply. Read the owner's manual carefully.

Much to my surprise, cancer <u>taught</u> me things. I didn't expect that. I've seen my life change, my priorities, and my attitude, and that has filled me with awe. In my fifties, when I was diagnosed, I never imagined that at that point in my life, I'd have my world turned upside down and have that turn out to be a good thing.

No. Cancer was **not** a good thing. Cancer did, however, bring me face-to-face with my mortality and through that, I learned to worry less and live more.

HOW I PERCEIVE MYSELF
BEING MORE AVAILABLE

What I gained in my soul has been priceless.

Insights Gained

1. To pursue deep emotional connections with people.

I found myself being interested on a different level. I wanted to connect with people, to be authentic and available.

2. To <u>experience</u> dreams, not just dream them.

I am taking chances. I've always dreamed of traveling in my golden years. I really wanted to see the Grand Canyon, for  example. It dawned on me that I didn't need to wait until retirement. What was I waiting on? None of us know how long we're on this earth, so why put off my dreams? Why put big dreams on a bucket list when we are unaware of when the bucket gets kicked? Why not <u>make</u> them happen at the first opportunity you can? So, that's what I did! Paul and I went to the Grand Canyon, and we have had many adventures since, some small and some large. I encourage you to do the same when feasible.

Please understand that I'm not advocating running up the plastic; practice good stewardship and start with day or weekend trips to get away to clear your mind and relax your body.

3. To reach out to other patients

I worked in the medical field and al-
ways cared about people. After cancer, there
was a deeper level of caring. It's hard to explain; it was just ... deeper. I've been meeting
people through online chats, organizations,
and groups, and it's become apparent that
there is a strong camaraderie among survivors. I've been meeting
people who have experienced the same struggles, treatments, side
effects, and emotions. I've learned to reach out and better connect.

4. To take opportunities – <u>just because</u>

There have been things in my life that I've had the opportunity to do but chose not to because they didn't seem to be a huge
priority, were too daunting, or I felt they simply weren't "me."
I'm taking those opportunities now. An example: A former employer had an annual Gala fundraiser. You know, one of those
events for the uppity-ups to get together and rub elbows. Some
want to go; others go because "it's expected of them." Everybody
at the facility receives an invitation to buy a ticket and get gussied
up, and everyone who "is someone" will be there. Well, one particular year, I went. Yep, me — who is so far from an "uppity-up"
went. Why? Why not? I had the opportunity; the ticket was provided for me, and my bonus daughter, Melissa, took on the challenge of making my very thin hair look respectable. She's truly a

miracle worker. The Gala was nice, and I didn't feel out of place because I apparently had more couth and culture than a lot of my small-town colleagues. (I tell myself that to amuse the refined me.)

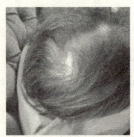
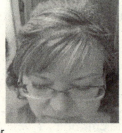

Before & After
my bonus daughter
worked miracles on
my hair

5. To prioritize, <u>differently</u>

PRIORITIES HAVE CHANGED

I never seemed to have a problem prioritizing. I do it differently now. Things that I fretted over (before cancer) aren't worth my worry now. If everything doesn't get ironed on Tuesday, so what? If I failed to pull weeds, who cares? If I cannot cook tonight, it's not a big deal. My husband had been trying for a long time to convince me that these things were trivial and that I shouldn't stress about them. I didn't seem to be able to adopt that attitude. Cancer changed that. It taught me to enjoy each day. I still prioritize, just differently. If something doesn't get done, it's okay;

tomorrow is another day, and EACH day should have joy. Sometimes, our joy gets buried underneath busyness and daily trials. Make it a point to grab joy with both hands, and don't let go. You'll find it in the most unlikely places: the eyes of a child, a phone call to a friend, a newly bloomed flower, a hug, taking a walk, or learning a new skill. There is joy in taking naps, too. Remember, there are no prizes for pushing through pain or stress, so lie down for a while. In my opinion, naps are highly underrated. <<wink>>

6. To become more <u>purpose-driven</u>

I'm living life with purpose now. Every day is a gift, and I appreciate that gift. I set more short-term goals. They're not large, unattainable goals but little things that mean something (to me or someone else).

7. To express <u>love</u> more openly.

I say "I love you" more frequently. I tell my family and my friends. I want to live without regret. I apologize when needed and show love as often as possible. That doesn't mean I can't be hurt; I certainly can. I've learned to try to walk away until the situation diffuses. Surprisingly, I've become more social, too. I see myself genuinely liking people, and kindness does indeed matter.

8. To <u>relax</u>

I've been through a lot of *opposites* in my life. There have been times when I was so skinny and, other times, significantly over-weight (like now). There were periods of abundant money and times when there was scarcely enough to live on. I've been loved

and resented. I've experienced both immense respect and moments of being belittled. My health is more important than any of those things, and I have learned to exhale and not be so uptight. Cancer has taught me that my identity is not in any of the above. I can relax and just be me.

I can relax and just be.

And that, my friends, is incredibly freeing.

9. To go beyond my <u>comfort zone</u>

Starting a blog was beyond my comfort zone. I never thought my life was so interesting or unique that I'd have any "hits" on the site. Now, I'm authoring a book, putting all my most sensitive and personal information on paper. This was WAY beyond my comfort zone. I've included incidents that I would NEVER have shared with the public. I've shared some very intimate things I wouldn't have ever shared with family members. But I've grown, and I've learned. I'm carefully moving outside the box for the greater good.

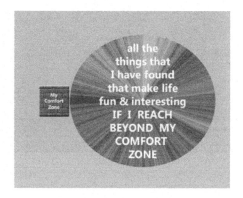

Chapter 17

LIFE EVER AFTER

Today, as I review the past and look toward the future, I am stepping into mile 1001. It's been a long and arduous journey. I thought, rethought and thought some more about everything that's happened. After all the embitterment, I questioned whether I would go through it all again. I found my answer with clarity and certainty as I sat cupping a large mug of cappuccino, sorting through miles of memories.

Photographs reminded me how much I would've missed had I not fought. I now know that I would go through it again. I realized my true worth through the amazing photo memories of the past ten years. The snapshots are of smiling people with joy on their faces and happiness in their hearts. I wasn't the only one smiling! Moments of incalculable value on the paper and ink. I had impacted their lives as much as they affected mine. What a profound revelation!

I came to recognize that I needed to support others through their battle. I found my "purpose," and it is to share my story and offer hope to fellow warriors and caregivers. After all this time, after all the fight, I found my ultimate "strength." I had become as strong as a garlic milkshake with my support system of family, friends and God. Furthermore, I learned how to live rather than to simply exist. These side effects can bite this old woman's treatment-damaged butt! I am thriving!

I have discovered how to (mostly) manage the long-term effects of treatments. I am pleased to report that many of my ugly presentations of sequelae have settled down, and a more normal way of life is now possible.

And now, I wish I could hold your hand and look at your face as I encourage you with the following.

1. Regardless of the stage or type of cancer that you or a loved one may be facing, fight it with all of your being.

   You and I are living stories; let's make them good ones.

2. Don't allow cancer to become your identity. It is not who you are. I refused to claim the cancer as <u>mine</u>. Always trying to be aware, I steered away from saying "my cancer." It wasn't MINE. I didn't own it.

   Cells mutated and divided aggressively within my body and tried to kill me, but I wouldn't take ownership of the disease. I now encourage you to do the same.

3. We are more powerful in numbers, so join a support group (even online ones have been a wealth of information and a source of strength for me). We can help each other.

We lift each other up when we are struggling. We share in triumphs, our hurts, and open our hearts. Private groups are a safe place to ask questions without concerns of judgment or fear of asking something embarrassing.

4. Pray. God does hear the prayers of His believers.

5. Be your own advocate. Speak up. And speak up again. You are worth it. Make sure your medical team sees you and knows you. They work for you, remember. Make decisions that are right for you.

    Your life depends on it.

6. Above all, don't lose hope. There is life after cancer, and it is worth living! Yes, the treatments can be brutal, but they are doable and I am living proof of that.

    Cancer was a beast, but so was I. There was a fight before me, and I chose to fight it. Going down <u>without</u> a fight wasn't an option. My family was not ever going to think, "Weren't we worth it?" or "Grandma didn't even give treatments a try," or "What if it was 'me' – wouldn't she want 'me' to fight?"

7. You will also take that first step into mile 1001. You have a positive impact to make. If you're through your journey, you fought the beast and survived.

Someone needs your help, insight, and knowledge to know they're not alone on their journey.

When it comes to living your after-cancer life, you don't have to write down everything you've ever wanted to do and try to accomplish it within the following year. If you do that, you'll be living to compete with a self-imposed chronograph, which will be stressful. Don't get so lost in chasing your bucket list that you lose sight of the extraordinary, ordinary moments.

Drink up life. Taste the sunshine. Feel your heartbeat. Inhale the future ahead of you. And hear what people say with their facial expressions.

I encourage you to enjoy being you. Make time for purposeful gatherings with those you care about.

For now, this content senior woman peacefully sits in her favorite rocking chair with bare feet. I smile as I reflect on cherished memories and extraordinary experiences. At this point in my life, I hope to radiate a sense of inner peace and wisdom, find joy in life's simple pleasures and cherish the company of friends and family. I want others to see me as a source of comfort and inspiration as they walk through their cancer journey.

As I often do, I dream about a coming time. I look forward to meeting you at mile marker 1002, where we can stroll together for a time. I will intently listen as you share your story with me. Make it a good one.

Chapter 18

GALLERY

A collection of photos that remind me of the time I spent in treatments. Now that I'm cancer-free, these photos serve as a reminder of how far I've come and how much my life has changed.

(Content warning: there are photos in the gallery of graphic procedures and the effects of medical treatment)

MY FAVORITE PHOTO OF MY SISTERS' SUPPORT

Trying on different wigs

Family is forever

Amazing …

**BEST GUY FRIEND
FOREVER, ROB**

**BEST GIRLFRIEND
FOREVER, DONNA**

… Friends

**BEST LONGTIME
FOREVER FRIEND,
SHELLEY**

**FRIENDS WHO PLANNED A
SPECIAL EVENT FOR DONNA
(ANN, JENNY, DONNA, ME &
EVA)**

Grandchildren
(faces covered for privacy and security)

and Great-grandchildren

Moments of Personal Growth

THE HAIRCUT BY SUNNY SABRINA

END OF TREATMENTS!

INDOOR SKYDIVING

THE DAY I GOT MY CONFIDENCE BACK

A SURVIVOR PARTY

Laura Zick-Mauzy

Chemo, Radiation & More

RADIATION SETTINGS

CHEMOTHERAPY

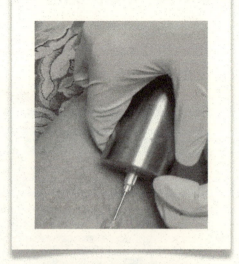

**INJECTION OF RADIOAC-
TIVE ISOTOPE (INTO MY
ARM) FOR A SCAN**

**SEVERE WEEPING
BURNS ON MY GROIN**

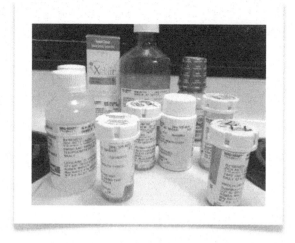

DAILY MEDICATIONS

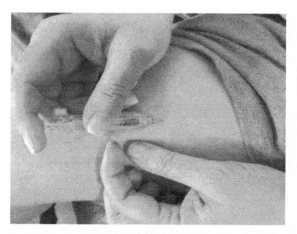

**INJECTING NEUPOGEN INTO
MY THIGH**

Memories ...

...with Paul

Glossary

5-fluorouracil- A type of chemotherapy drug.

ACA – The Affordable Care Act (also known as Obama-care). An alternative to traditional healthcare insurance as it is a subsidy available to those with lower incomes.

Acute lymphocytic leukemia - A rapidly growing cancer of white blood cells (specifically, lymphocytes).

Antidepressant - A drug that is used to reduce feelings of sadness, worry, and hopelessness. It helps by balancing the chemicals in the brain.

Antimetabolite – A substance that interferes with the metabolism of other cells. As a cancer treatment, it interferes with the replication of cancer cells.

Anus - The opening at the end of the intestines through which solid excrement leaves the body. It's the last inch or so of the GI (gastrointestinal) tract.

Anxiety - An uncomfortable feeling of nervousness or worry about something that is happening or might happen in the future.

Bidet seat - A combination of a toilet and wash basin used to clean the lower trunk of the body after voiding or defecating.

Bile acid - The primary acid in bile that plays a role in lipid metabolism. Too much bile acid in the colon can cause "chronic diarrhea" because of malabsorption.

Biofeedback - A mind-body control technique that involves learning to control a physical or mental process using information from recordings of those processes.

A biopsy - This is removing and examining a small amount of tissue from a sick person to discover more about their illness. The biopsies are then sent to the pathology department to be analyzed.

Bladder - An organ like a bag inside the body of a person or animal, where urine is stored before it leaves the body.

C. diff – An abbreviation for Clostridium difficile: a bacterium that can cause serious illness with diarrhea, colitis, and dehydration. It can be challenging to treat and is highly contagious.

Cancer - A severe disease caused when cells in the body grow uncontrollably and abnormally. These mutated cells begin killing normal cells, and this disease can cause death.

Carcinoma - A cancerous growth that forms on or inside the body.

Chemo - See chemotherapy

Chemotherapy - The treatment of diseases using chemicals. There are numerous ways to receive chemo (infusion, pills, etc.).

Clostridium difficile - See C. diff.

Colonoscopy - A medical examination of the colon.

Depression - A mental illness in which a person is very unhappy and anxious for long periods and cannot have a normal life during these periods. A trauma, stress, a side effect of medication, etc. can trigger it.

Dilator - A device used to stretch vaginal walls after stenosis.

Estrogen - A female hormone that causes development and change in the reproductive organs.

Farrah Fawcett - An iconic American actress (1947-2009) who succumbed to anal cancer.

Fine needle aspiration – A procedure to remove a liquid or gas from a space in the body using a fine needle.

Flex sigmoid – See Flexible sigmoidoscopy.

Flexible sigmoidoscopy – A medical examination of the lower part of the colon. The physician uses a long, narrow (flexible) tube with a light on it to examine the rectum and lower colon. This procedure does not reach the upper colon.

FMLA – An abbreviation for Family Medical Leave Act (of 1993). It is a U.S. law to see that employees are provided with up to twelve weeks of unpaid leave and job protection. Specific criteria must be met to be approved.

Genital warts – Small bumps on the genitals caused by an infection of the HPV.

HIV – An abbreviation for human immunodeficiency virus: the virus that causes AIDS.

Hot spots – A term for places on a PET/CT scan that appear to glow are called hot spots. They can indicate cancer cell growth.

HPV – An abbreviation for human papillomavirus- which is a large group of viruses, some of which can cause warts and cancers in the genital areas. A vaccine is available.

Human immunodeficiency virus – see HIV

Human papilloma virus – see HPV

Incontinence – The inability to control the excretion of urine or the contents of the bowels.

Infusion – Adding one substance into the body through a vein over a few hours.

Intravenous – Inside the veins. (See IV)

Invasive – A medical term describing cancer cells moving aggressively into a nearby healthy tissue area.

IV – An abbreviation for intravenous. A method of administering a substance into a vein.

Kegel – Is an exercise that involves squeezing the muscles in your pelvis and holding them tight for a few seconds.

Laser beam – A powerful, narrow line of light used to perform medical procedures.

Latent – The status of being present (but hidden and without symptoms) with the capability of developing into an active state. Dormancy.

Laxative – A substance that makes it easier for the waste from someone's bowels to come out.

Leg mold – A device formed to fit the legs very closely.

Lethargy – Thefeeling of having little energy or being unable or unwilling to do anything.

Lidocaine – A drug used as a local anesthetic.

Lymph – A clear liquid transports useful substances around the body and carries waste matter, such as un-wanted bacteria, away from body tissue to prevent infection.

Lymphedema – A condition in which body tissues be-come swollen because lymph cannot be carried away from them.

Magnetic resonance imaging – See MRI

Malabsorption – A disorder that prevents nutrients from being absorbed through the small intestine.

Mitomycin – A type of chemotherapy drug.

MRI – An abbreviation for magnetic resonance imaging, a system for producing electronic pictures of the organs inside a person's body using radio waves and a strong magnetic field.

Mutated – When speaking of cells, mutated cells have undergone a change because their DNA has been altered. When the mutation tells the cells to divide uncontrollably, cancer can develop.

Neupogen – A medication in the drug class of colony-stimulating factors. It stimulates the bone marrow to produce more white blood cells, boosting a weakened immune system.

Neurologist – A doctor who studies and treats diseases of the nerves.

Neurology – The study of the structure and diseases of the brain and all the nerves in the body.

Neuropathy – Damage to or disease affecting the nerves. Symptoms can include pins and needles, pain, weakness, or even numbness.

Nigro protocol – The current standard of care for anal cancer, which includes chemotherapy (mitomycin and 5-fluorouracil) with radiotherapy. Named after Norman Nigro.

Oncologist – A doctor who specializes in cancers of the body.

Oncology – The study and treatment of tumors in the body.

Oropharyngeal – The part of the throat behind the mouth. It includes the back part of the tongue, the tonsils, the soft palate, and the portion of the mouth on each side of the uvula.

Osteopenia – A condition of bone loss. It affects more women than men.

Palpate – The process of using hands or fingers to examine something, usually an organ or part of the body.

Pathologist – An expert in the study of diseases.

Pathology – The scientific study of disease.

Peripheral neuropathy – Damage to the nerves that connect the brain and spinal cord to the extremities.

PET Scan – An abbreviation for positron emission to-mography scan, which is a medical test that produces an image of the brain or another part of a person's body. It uses a radioactive tracer to show how the body and organs work. Diseases can be seen on this type of scan.

PICC line – An abbreviation for peripherally inserted central catheter line. A small tube (catheter) is positioned centrally (near the heart) and inserted through a vein in the upper (peripheral) arm. It can be used for medication, nutri-ents, blood draws, etc.

Plantar wart – This is a small, hard, infectious, seed-like growth on the skin, usually on the bottom of the foot. HPV causes it.

Platelets – These are tiny cells in the blood that make it thicker and more solid to stop bleeding caused by an in-jury.

PLS – An abbreviation for Primary Lateral Sclerosis, a rare neuromuscular disease that weakens muscles and slows movement.

Polyp - A small mass of cells that grows in the body and is not usually harmful.

Post-traumatic embitterment disorder – A
mental condition in which a person suffers severe and prolonged embitterment, anger, helplessness, and self-blame. This can occur as a reaction to an intensely adverse life event.

Prayer shawl – A shawl made for someone that will
be given as a gift. The shawl maker begins with prayers and blessings for the recipient. Upon completion of the shawl, a final blessing is offered before the shawl is sent to someone undergoing medical procedures as a comfort after a loss or in times of stress. They are also called comfort shawls, mantles, or peace shawls.

Psychiatrist – A doctor who specializes in mental
health.

PTSD – An abbreviation for Post Traumatic Stress Disorder.
It is a mental condition in which a person suffers severe anxiety and depression after a very frightening or shocking experience, such as an accident or a war. One common symptom is vivid flashbacks.

PTO – An abbreviation for Paid Time Off (sometimes
known as PDO – Paid Days Off).

Radiation (therapy) – The use of controlled amounts of radiation to treat disease in a particular body part. There is internal and external radiation.

Radiation enteritis – Damage to the intestines caused by radiotherapy, resulting in pain and diarrhea.

Radiation-induced lumbar plexopathy – see RILP.

Rectum – The lowest end of the bowels, down which solid waste travels before leaving the body through the anus.

Relay for Life – This is an annual cancer charity walk sponsored by the American Red Cross. It raises awareness, celebrates survivors, remembers loved ones, and raises money for continued research.

Replication – The act of a cell using its DNA to make exact copies of itself.

RILP – An abbreviation for Radiation-Induced Lumbar Plexopathy; A rare and severe condition of damaged nerves caused by pelvic radio-chemotherapy treatments. This can interfere with walking and daily life (numbness and foot drop).

Sarcoma – A cancerous lump in the bones, muscles, or joints.

Silvadine cream – Silver sulphadiazine antimicrobial cream used for burns and wounds.

Soft tissue – Any tissue but bone. It is a group of connected cells in a living organism (plant or animal) that are similar to each other, have the same purpose, and form the stated part of the animal or plant.

Sphincter – A muscle that surrounds an opening in the body and can tighten to close it. There are many sphincters throughout the body.

Squamous cells – The type of cells that make up the outer and middle layers of skin.

Stage – A classification of disease progression upon diagnosis.

Stenosis – A part of a passage or opening in the body that has become abnormally narrow, or the act of this happening.

Stigma – Is a strong disapproval that most people in a society have about something. It is typically unfair and associated with shaming.

Stress fractures – A thin crack in a bone, especially in the leg or foot.

Thoracotomy – A surgical procedure where there is a cut into the wall of the chest between two ribs. This procedure is done for diagnosis or treatment.

Thymus – A small gland behind the breastbone that helps build the immune system.

Tubular adenoma – A precancerous polyp found in the colon or rectum.

Tumor – A mass of cells in the body that grows faster than usual and may or may not be malignant.

Vaccine – A substance that is put into the body to protect them from a disease by causing them to produce antibodies.

Vesicant – A substance only given through the vein because it will cause blistering when administered outside the vein.

Virus – A tiny piece of organic material that causes disease in humans, animals, and plants.

WBC – An abbreviation for White Blood Cell.

X-ray – A type of radiation that can penetrate many solid substances, allowing hidden objects such as bones and organs to be photographed.